ST UCK

Pull your God-Given Dreams Into Reality

Sheri Yates

Publisher iKAN Publishing
Stuck
Copyright (c) 2013 by Sheri Yates

This title is also available as a Kindle e-book.

I would love to hear from you. Send your comments to
stuck@ikanministries.com
This title may also be purchased from ikanministries.com/stuck.html

ISBN-10: 1479135410
ISBN-13: 9781479135417

All Scripture quotations, unless otherwise indicated, are taken
from the Holy Bible, New International Version 1984 (NIV). Other
Scripture references are from the King James Version (KJV), New
American Standard Bible (NASB), New Living Translation (NLT),
and the New King James Version (NKJV). All emphasis added.

Sheri Yates is represented by iKAN Ministries, Edmond, Oklahoma.

Cover and Interior design: CreateSpace
Editor: Trisha Heddlesten
Photos: Micah Marie Photography

Printed in the United States of America

ACKNOWLEDGMENTS

Writing a book is no easy task. It's one thing to have the idea; it's a whole other thing to stick legs on it!

The cover of this book says I am the author, but in reality, it was authored by many. I am so grateful for the countless hours my family imagined with me, wrote parts of this book, and encouraged me.

I thank my God and Savior Jesus Christ for picking me up from a life of destruction, making me whole, and setting me free so I could pursue His plans for me!

Spencer, Chandler, and Kennedi—I love you girls so much! I wrote *Stuck* to pass on the revelation God has given me to future generations so you could maybe, *just maybe*, learn from my hard-knocks rather than your own. Thank you for loving me and believing in me! I am so grateful that I am your mom!

Thank you to Trisha Heddlesten, who is a word ninja. She gave *order* to my haphazard words and arranged them to sound intelligent.

Thank you especially to my husband, TY. He spent countless hours working through edits with me when my desire for perfection became a burden to the process. He is my tireless warrior!

I'm thankful for my friend and sister Kathleen. She was available at any moment to help me with research or to offer a detailed critique, and she was a crucial part of finishing this book. She encouraged me to never give up.

Elizabeth and Kathleen, thank you for inspiring me to write *Stuck*.

I thank my pastors, Craig and Amy Groeschel, for relentlessly encouraging, not only me, but also our entire Church to step out in faith!

DEDICATION

*Stuck is dedicated to all who have settled in
life and given up on their dreams.
May God turn you upside down and revive
His visions in you!*

* * *

*Stuck is also dedicated to my girls, Spencer,
Chandler and Kennedi.
I wrote this so that if your dreams are ever crushed
and stuck you would know how to revive them.
God has mighty plans for your life.
Plans to prosper you, give you a future.
Plans to help you not to harm you in any way!
May God have your heart always!*

CONTENTS

INTRODUCTION

Tim was a security guard where my husband and I worked. He was a great guy. He loved his kids and although his English was a little rough, he loved America. Tim was ambitious. He had big visions and in his 40's he was relentlessly pursuing a college degree while working multiple jobs and learning English. His child-like faith in his future inspired us. He was a big thinker and an extraordinary dreamer!

One Friday on my way out of the office, Tim was heavily on my mind after our typical – *what's going on in your world this weekend* – conversation. I knew I needed to ask him a specific question, but I didn't interrupt my desperate desire to flee the office that late Friday evening. Early Monday morning I learned Tim had been shot and killed while providing security at a business. I would never know the answer to my question. Had Tim accepted Jesus Christ as his Lord and Savior? Would I meet my incredible, intellectual, ambitious friend again in Heaven?

I hope you will read this book and be inspired to freely envision your faith-filled dreams and become unstoppable in your pursuit. Moreover to infinity, I need to know your answer to the question I never asked Tim – *"Do you know Jesus Christ as your Lord and Savior? Will I be with you again someday?"*

Did you have hopes for your future when you were a child? Maybe your mom saved a paper from your childhood, as my mom did, on which you wrote, *"When I grow up, I want to be a ..."* My paper read, *"When I grow up, I hope to be an actress, singer, and dancer."*

Maybe you daydreamed you were a professional athlete, a gourmet chef, a full-time missionary, or a member of Congress. Perhaps your vision was to learn a foreign language or mentor someone younger than you—or write a book! Are you living your purpose today? If so, this book probably isn't for you!

But if you have given up on God's calling or aren't sure how to take the first step in pursuing God's plans for you then you are reading the right book! If you know your purpose, but need motivation to start, you are reading the right book! Ready to recapture the courage to pursue your dreams?

When did you stop aspiring to do more? Have your hopes been crushed by a well-meaning friend or family member? When my mom read my "When I grow up...." kindergarten paper, she was not inspired to enroll me in dance, music classes, or singing lessons. Both of my parents worked full-time to barely earn a living so we didn't have the money for extracurricular activities. We were broke, broke, broke—like, beans-for-dinner broke.

No one in my family had ever had a successful career in singing, acting, or dancing. To my parents, those were careers that would lead me to being...*broke*. They desired that I would have a better life than they had. They hoped I would earn enough money to support myself well. In their opinion, encouraging my fantasies would lead me down a path to certain failure and living at home forever!

Not many of us grow up considering, *I would love it if I never made enough money to move out and stand on my own two feet.* I certainly did not. I aspired to move out as early as fifteen years old. Before I had the chance to start and fail, my parents shot down my young career choices with the daunting facts that I would never earn the wages necessary to support myself, I began to pursue other things. I looked for "a decent job" with "decent pay," one that was familiar, safe, and risk-free. Guess what I chose? Accounting. Yes, I did. It is amazing how far away I catapulted myself from my original intent!

Somehow, I made it through college, but in my career, almost everyone I worked with couldn't believe I was an accountant because I didn't have the personality of a "typical" number-cruncher. *Duh!* That should have been a huge red flag.

My God-given design isn't for accounting! I am an extrovert. I love people. I can *barely* stand *details*.

Although they had the best intentions, my parents killed my dreams. What about your parents? What about you? If you are guilty of killing someone's big vision, you might be a dream killer.

> Before we proceed, I need to clarify one thing—I am not condoning encouraging your loved ones to blindly jump in with both feet to every wild and risky whim. Before you close this book, assuming, *this lady has her head in the clouds,* please understand that this process of pursuing your dreams is more about relationship than results. It is a discovery of your dreams one tiny step at a time. As you and your loved ones begin the steps, God is the one who opens the doors and guides your feet into His path for you! Proverbs 3:5-6 reveals that God directs our steps. This verse assumes that we are stepping.

When you discourage other people's desires with your opinions, you are probably looking at the possible results rather than how doing so will impact your relationship. When you shoot down people's dreams before they even try, they are less likely to share the deepest desires of their heart with you again. But when you listen and respond with positive affirmation, your relationship is inevitably going to be strengthened. Instead of killing the passion with reasoning, *Stuck* will set you free to follow God quickly. It is a journey to climb out of the rut and into the dreams God has for your life.

> **You were born with a plan. It's like a birthmark—it's part of who you are.**

You no longer need to live *Stuck*. I have a tool for you to get out of the rut: The *Stickie Dreamwall*! It's a process that guides you by taking baby steps toward the ideas God has placed in your heart. You will begin with learning to dream again. We will discover lies that prevent us from pursuing our God-given dreams. You will pray over your dreams and ask God to direct your steps. By the end of this book, you will be taking steps toward accomplishing at least one dream God has called you to do!

If someone in your family has a vision that is, on the surface, far-fetched or destined for failure, remember that there are countless small actions between exploration and fulfillment of that dream. In time, either God will open doors in a miraculous way, refocus the dreamer's desire, or reveal that the dream was not from Him.

When you are open to the *Stickie Dreamwall* process, you open your heart and life to be the stage on which

God can work in amazing ways. Whether you realize it or not, God has already placed a dream in your heart. You were born with it. It's similar to a birthmark—it's part of who you are. You were born with a plan and an identity. Many never discover it. Be the one who does! Read on.

———

So, why is it so important to recover the forgotten or ignored dreams God has placed in our hearts? Because in pursuing those dreams, we are pursuing a closer relationship with God, living out His purpose for our lives, and positively impacting the world around us.

Often, we find ourselves troubled by circumstances in the world around us, not realizing that God has given us eyes to see a particular problem because we are the people to carry His solution to the world. The objective of the *Stickie Dreamwall* process is to help you identify, ignite, and execute the dreams in your heart—and in our world.

Too many of God's children have shrunk back into a seat of comfort and contentment rather than taken up the cause of Christ. As a result, way too many people who are suffering, in bondage, and without truth end up dying without knowing the love of God.

But we are not of those who shrink back and are destroyed, but of those who believe and are saved
(HEBREWS 10:39).

If we aren't doing our job as believers, it's because we are in bondage to something—insecurity, over commitments, comfort, or fear of people's opinions about us—but God has a dream for you! It's a dream that will impact your life and the lives of many others. Do you know what it is? Have you done anything about it? Well, this book is a kick in the pants to get you started!

God wants His children to dream and imagine again so He can use us fully to fulfill His purposes on this earth!

The harvest is plentiful, but the workers are few
(LUKE 10:2).

God is looking for those who hunger to work in His fields doing the work He has designed them for and called them to do. By the end of this book, I pray you'll be asking, imagining, and dreaming from the very heart of God again. God longs for His children to dream and imagine so He can use us fully to fulfill His purposes on this earth!

Engage your faith and set your mind to get out of your comfort zone. You may have to stop doing something good to start experiencing God's best for your life.

Father, form me to be usable. Flood my eyes and ears to hear your great plans for me.

*I give you permission to ignite your dreams
in my heart. In Jesus name, Amen.*

———

I would *love* to hear from you. Please send your comments to stuck@ikanministries.com.

Part 1

IDENTIFYING THE PROBLEM

Chapter 1

YOU MIGHT BE A DREAM KILLER

*"All our dreams come true if we have the
courage to pursue them."*

~ WALT DISNEY

So many people have learned to suppress or ignore their dreams over time. Why is this? What are the factors that discourage us from pursuing our dreams? In the next few chapters, we will explore the reasons people abandon their dreams over time. Hopefully, in identifying the elements of the problem, we can move past them and learn to become dreamers again. People generally fall into one of three categories: dream killers, dream keepers, or dream lifters.

Dream killers respond to a dream with these type conclusions: What if, I can't, I shouldn't, or never. They fear failure more than they know and fear God. Their faith is in what they can see with their physical eyes, which reflects how little they trust God. Their lack of faith limits God's ability to develop His dreams in their life.

> **The Dream Killer makes no progress because he imagines the worst possible outcome.**

Dream keepers have big dreams but get little accomplished. They believe they can accomplish great things but still fear failure at their core. They trust God only in the things they know for sure will not result in failure.

Dream lifters recognize the full power of the cross. They intentionally stay outside their comfort zone because they trust in God. They encourage others into action with their excitement and hope for life in Christ!

Which category do you identify with? Many of us would love to be a dream lifter but find hesitation driven by practicality, and the influence of others holds us back from pursuing God's dreams for our lives.

———

To better understand the types of dreamers, let's look at these personalities in action. Jesus told a parable about what three men did with gifts they were given by their master. This story is an excellent illustration of the three styles.

A man traveled on a journey and entrusted his wealth to three of his servants. The first one received five bags of gold, the second two bags, and the third one.

The servant with five bags immediately invested it wisely. The man given two bags also put it to use, but more cautiously. The third servant dug a hole and buried his bag of gold. When the master returned, he settled his accounts with the servants. Let's look at how the master responded to their use of His gifts:

> *"The man who had received the five talents brought the other five. 'Master,' he said, 'you entrusted me with five talents. See, I have gained five more.' His master replied, 'Well done, good and faithful servant! You have been faithful with a few things; I will put you in charge of many things. Come and share your master's happiness!'"*

> *"The man with the two talents also came. 'Master,' he said, 'you entrusted me with two talents; see, I have gained two more.' His master replied, 'Well done, good and faithful servant! You have been faithful with a few things; I will put you in charge of many things. Come and share your master's happiness!'"*

"Then the man who had received the one talent came. 'Master,' he said, 'I knew that you are a hard man, harvesting where you have not sown and gathering where you have not scattered seed. So I was afraid and went out and hid your talent in the ground. See, here is what belongs to you.' His master replied, 'You wicked, lazy servant! So you knew that I harvest where I have not sown and gather where I have not scattered seed? Well then, you should have put my money on deposit with the bankers, so that when I returned I would have received it back with interest. Take the talent from him and give it to the one who has the ten talents.'"

"For everyone who has will be given more, and he will have an abundance. Whoever does not have, even what he has will be taken from him. And throw that worthless servant outside, into the darkness, where there will be weeping and gnashing of teeth" (Matthew 25:16–30).

What have you done with the dreams and gifts God has placed in your possession? Each of us has received unique gifts from God. What you do with the talents He has given you is entirely up to you.

The servant who received one bag of gold was a dream killer. He didn't really know or trust his master. He believed what he had heard, and it made him fear his master's wrath. His interest was in protecting himself from harm. His selfishness prevented him from investing. Perhaps he dwelt on past failures. The dream killer makes no progress because he imagines the worst possible outcome.

Dream killers rely on their own understanding more than God. False humility is their cover for their pride in knowing what's best for them. They only have faith in the results, which reflects how little they trust God. They are a direct reflection of the man who buried his talents because of fear of his master's punishment. If you don't know God intimately, then you cannot truly trust Him and your fear will kill the dreams He has placed in you.

The man who invested two bags of gold was a dream keeper. He saw himself with great success and was proud of the result he delivered. However, he really didn't know and trust his master, so he was only willing to invest in a sure thing. The dream keeper is only willing to invest in a guaranteed result. His actions overflow out of what he knows, understands, and comprehends. His master still rewards his tiny faith, but the investor is oblivious to the fact that his self-preserving actions only limit his opportunity to serve the master.

Dream keepers are inspired by great people of action and view themselves inwardly with this greatness, but they still fear failure in their hearts. They will only take "risks" that have a secured, positive conclusion. They are the reflection of the man who cautiously invested the two bags of gold. They are often critical of other people, lead-

> **The Dream Keeper is only willing to invest in a guaranteed result.**

ers, and processes, predicting all probable downfalls rather than potential benefits of an action. They have more wisdom and drive than dream killers, but they still don't fully trust God.

The servant who received the five bags of gold was a dream lifter. He knew and trusted his master, so he was willing to risk everything to serve him. He was not concerned with himself or afraid of hard work, and most likely, his past experience with serving the master had proven successful. His hope carried his imagination.

Dream lifters inspire people! Their enthusiasm rubs off on those around them and they motivate others into action without trying. They recognize the full power of the cross and realize that forgiveness and eternal salvation are larger than anything happening in their world. They have a deep understanding of God's love and power. They invest without fear, knowing that it is God who will bring a good return on their obedience. They stay outside their comfort zone because they know

> **The Dream Lifter is willing to risk everything to serve the master.**

that miracles happen in rough water—they have experienced God in action. They notice people for their potential rather than their current status. They detect themselves in others. They know the same God who raised them from the dead can lift anyone with a desire for change and a mustard seed of hope through a mountain of adversity.

Which are you: a dream keeper, dream killer, or dream lifter? Commit to obtaining God's truth.

If you are a dream killer, we are going to identify what is suppressing your ability to dream. Is it fear? Failure? Loss of hope? Negative influences? Sometimes the idea of these things can crush a goal. We will talk about these more in depth in the next chapter.

Are you a dream keeper with big dreams and little action? Ask God to reveal where you might not fully know his love and power in your life. Ask those around you to help you identify blind spots where you might not trust God.

If you are a dream lifter who trusts God and you are executing on your dreams if only in small ways—celebrate! Whether you have achieved tangible results is not important. Faith is built by trusting God and taking action without fear of failure.

God is able to do more than you can think, ask, imagine, or dream. But what is it that you are contemplating, dreaming, and imagining? Is it big enough for God?

Now to him who is able to do immeasurably more than all we ask or imagine, according to his power that is at work within us.

~ EPHESIANS 3:20

Chapter 2

FEAR CAN BE STICKY

"If we are dominated by fear, then we cannot operate in faith."

~ PERRY NOBLE

I have shared the *Stickie Dreamwall* process at conferences and our family has shared it with many families in their living rooms. We consistently note that young children are fabulous, on-fire dreamers! Young adults are quieter and more reserved. They are hesitant to share and seem shy or embarrassed to announce their dreams openly. Adults are a mixed bag. Sometimes, we get the ones who don't dream at all for themselves, and other times we meet those who are still dreaming machines. That doesn't mean, however, that they have taken a single step toward accomplishing those dreams.

My husband and I often contemplate what has to occur to turn the free, young-spirited dreamer into the reserved teen / young adult, and finally the pessimistic adult. *What point in our lives are our dreams suppressed?*

I am going to draw from the Bible to suggest three life events that often suppress our ability to dream: fear, previous failures, and loss or devastation.

Fear

Fear can keep you from falling asleep at night. Many dream-quenching fears are founded in the what-if questions. When you hear that the econ-

Fear limits freedom.

omy is tanking, your mind is immediately filled with worries of layoffs at your company, not enough money for family necessities, and mounting bills. Fear can keep you from trying out for the team. Fear of rejection can hold you back from new relationships. When you have the opportunity to step into a new leadership role, your mind can turn to scenes of you making a fool of yourself or collapsing under the pressure. Fear causes us to imagine the worst-case scenario.

Fear will always keep you from walking in total freedom. Harboring fear will cause you to trust in things and circumstances, rather than God. My pastor, and one of my favorite authors, Craig Groeschel, phrases it this way: "What you fear reveals what you value most. What you fear reveals where you trust God least."

Many things can cause fear, but I have seen that the kind of fear that holds a person back from pursuing his or her dreams generally falls into these three categories:

- Fear you may not succeed
- Fear of what will happen to you, your family, or your livelihood
- Fear of other people's opinions about you

Jesus' last words to His disciples begin in John 14. He was about to be crucified and was preparing the disciples for the upcoming turmoil. He longed for them to be strong and unmoved by their circumstances. Jesus desired that they would stand firm in what he had taught them over the last three years.

Jesus commanded the disciples not to allow emotions and negative circumstances to control their behavior with the words, *"Do not let your heart be troubled"* (John 14:1, 27 *paraphrased*).

Seriously? They were about to witness the beating and death of their leader, friend, and teacher.

Did they follow His instructions? Nope. They ran in fear and trembling. Because they didn't have a full understanding of God's plan, in that moment, it appeared they had wasted the past three years of their lives. Their fear was greater than their trust in Jesus.

If your dreams are suppressed because of fear, then face it—you are not trusting God in this area of your life.

In trust, our imaginations are our greatest strength in reaching for God's dreams for us. In fear, our imaginations are the greatest hurdle working against us.

I was born with a severe swayback; the doctors told my parents I would never be able to be a dancer or a gymnast. When they told me that I couldn't dance because of this defect, in my imagination, I immediately saw myself with a crippling inability. I couldn't imagine myself as a healed overcomer. As a child, I didn't try to dance because of the fear of becoming crippled.

When I finally did become a dancer at the age of eighteen, I was shocked to find that I was naturally very good at it. I actually had a little talent! A gift. I had missed it because fear had crippled me.

In Exodus 16, after the Israelites escaped slavery in Egypt, they wandered in the wilderness and worried about what they would eat. They were afraid of dying and did not trust the Lord to provide for them. They wanted to return to slavery and return to their comfort zone because of fear. They were stuck in a negative mind-set and quit dreaming of God's Promised Land, the land flowing with milk and honey.

> *In the desert the whole community grumbled*
> *against Moses and Aaron. The Israelites said*
> *to them, "If only we had died by the Lord's*

hand in Egypt! There we sat around pots
of meat and ate all the food we wanted, but
you have brought us out into this desert
to starve this entire assembly to death"
(Exodus 16:2–3).

Pray about it and ask God to reveal to you three things you fear the most that might be holding you back from pursuing the dreams God has placed on your heart.

Fear can be sticky. Don't let fear prevent you from pursuing God's dreams for you.

Failure

I spoke at a Bible study in which I had everyone hold up a sign that represented an area in which he or she was struggling in life. My eleven-year-old daughter was one of the participants. She chose the sign: *failure*.

> **"One mistake does not have to rule a person's entire life."**
> **~ JOYCE MEYER**

Later, I asked her why she had chosen that particular sign. She shared that daily she struggles with the fear of failing. When half of her math work is incorrect or when she argues with a sister or if she forgets to brush her teeth, she mentally beats herself up. Why are we so hard on ourselves? Why do we let small defeats haunt us?

Maybe you actually had the guts and took the risk to start a business, but it flopped. You tried. It failed. So you quit. Failure is a dream killer. Feelings of failure, whether it's true or not, will prevent you from ever trying anything new. One of my favorite authors, Joyce Meyer, stated, "One mistake does not have to rule a person's entire life." How true!

A friend of ours didn't allow failure to kill his dream. His first restaurant failed, but he took what he learned from his mistakes and tried again. What nerve! How could he risk his family's livelihood again? He could have focused on the negative what-if questions, but instead, he decided that he would be much more likely to succeed the second time because of what he had gained from the first attempt. Today, he runs one of the most successful restaurants in our city! He did not allow failure to kill his dreams. No, he allowed failure to teach and fuel him.

In the books Ezra and Nehemiah, failure prevailed in Jerusalem because the enemy had torn down their city walls. The Israelites attempted to rebuild the wall to protect their community and their families, but they failed. When they looked at their crumbling wall, they must have been concluding, *There's no way we can ever do this*. They were defeated by their own failures. They did not pursue God for a solution. Instead, the people of Jerusalem chose to live in constant fear of an enemy attack on their unprotected city.

Do you ever feel that way? Are you crippled by fear? Does your fear of failure spawn other fears in your life? Are you constantly vulnerable to attack because of this continual state of self-doubt?

Dwelling on your past failures will always prevent you from noticing what God is doing today! If you are stuck in the past, it's time to leave it behind. Really. Why would we choose to allow the past to control our future? My ten-year-old daughter says, with wisdom beyond her years, "The past is trash. Leave it there."

> ## *"When you are tempted to give up, your breakthrough is probably just around the corner."*
> ~ JOYCE MEYER

I love that word of encouragement, because it is most often true!

What are at least two failures from your past that changed your present circumstances? Pray and ask God to uncover any lies that you may believe about yourself as a result of these failures. Ask Him to cover and replace these lies with His truth about you.

Failure is only preparation for future success!

Loss/Devastation

In 1 Samuel 30, David and his men returned from war to find that their wives, children, and possessions had been stolen. Everything was lost.

Imagine if you dashed home today to find your family was gone. House burned. Children taken. You were all alone...I do not wish to minimize this because many may have lost someone you deeply loved. In fact, Cheli Porter knows all too well what David and his men experienced. She personally lived every mother's worst nightmare. In one moment, she lost everything. Her ex-husband murdered her three sons and then himself.

While I was writing *Stuck*, I deeply considered Cheli's story. *How could a person live on after a loss of this magnitude?* Oh, how I grieved for her.

Can you imagine yourself in her shoes? How would you feel? How would you react? After you are finished picking yourself up from the pain you are feeling, read on.

David and his men wept. They wept until they were exhausted. These men grieved until they could no longer cry.

After their grieving, the men became angry. They directed their anger at their leader, David. I envision this giant "hissy-fit!" I can hear them saying "He led us into war. He brought us back to this devastation. It's all *his* fault. Let's get 'em!" They wanted to kill David. Through the pain of their loss, they lost hope that their situation could be restored. The devastating circumstances limited their ability to observe with faith and dream God's dreams!

"When things go wrong, don't go with them."

~ ELVIS PRESLEY

So what happened to my friend Cheli? Within the first twenty-four hours after she heard about the death of her three sons, she determined not to ask God why; she realized she was still on Earth for a purpose and asked God to lead her to it. She came to this conclusion within a day of this tremendous loss!

She reminds me of David, because that is what he did! *"David was greatly distressed because the men were talking of stoning him; each one was bitter in spirit because of his sons and daughters. But David found strength in the LORD his God"* (1 Samuel 30:6). After he encouraged himself in the Lord, he sought God for a plan to take back what had been stolen!

David lifted the morale of an entire army of six hundred men and inspired them to have faith that God would give them the final victory. Those men rallied and took back 100 percent of what had been stolen from them, plus all the wealth of their enemy.

We can allow loss and devastation to prevent progress. Living in the past, prevents us from being aware of God's work today. With God's plan, we are always victorious!

Moving On

Maybe your dreams have been lost or suppressed because of fear, past failures, or loss. *Stuck* is going to help restore your God-given dreams! It's not too late. Keep pressing through the pages. Let God stir you and help you realize you are worthy to do what He's called you to!

Release past failures, fears, and despair. Give it all to God. Today. Listen to God, and you can become a dream lifter!

Where there is no vision, the people perish.

~ PROVERBS 29:18 KJV

Chapter 3

STUCK IN A NEGATIVE MIND-SET

"Stop being tormented by everyone else's reaction to you."

~ JOYCE MEYER

If it's not a past full of fear, failure, or loss that is keeping you from being a dream lifter, it could be a pessimistic pattern that prevents you from opening your life to God's dreams for you.

Sometimes we get stuck in a negative mind-set because of our own internal assessment, and other times, we are influenced by the opinions of others. Maybe you have a dream of owning your own business, but when you share your idea with friends, they give you many reasons why it wouldn't work. They might pose questions like, "What if it fails and you lose your entire life savings?" This could get you focused on the worst-case scenario. The obstacles that well-meaning friends and family present often prevent us from pursuing our dreams. Before you know it, all you have is a dead dream.

Maybe that's you? Maybe your parents bombarded your dreams with real-life issues.

> *"You have to pay the rent."*
> *"You need a 'secure' job to provide for a family."*
> *"You can't possibly risk the livelihood of your family for a dream. You gave that up when you started having kids."*
> *"You are not that smart."*
> *"It didn't work last time."*

Some people will never believe in your God-given dreams.

> **"I could never convince the financiers that Disneyland was feasible, because dreams offer too little collateral."**
> **~ WALT DISNEY**

Grace's Story

Grace had a wake up call when she realized she was a dream killer. When her son was twelve years old, he would not stay on task with his schoolwork. He would sneak off, and Grace assumed he wanted to avoid working. After she grounded him from his two favorite things—"the great outdoors" and "things that plug in"—he brought her the project he had been sneaking off to invent: a portable charger for Grace's phone. He told her, "Mom, you know how your phone always goes dead when you're out because you forget to charge it? Well, now you can carry this in your purse and plug your phone into it so you don't miss calls."

Grace shared, "He had figured out the correct wattage so it would not mess up my phone and he actually made it attractive, too. I began to meditate on my mantra: *I will not be a dream killer. I will not be a dream killer.* I have tried to encourage his [gift for] inventing even when there are little wires everywhere or things taken apart."

———

Although we desire the best for our kids, friends, spouse, and peers, without knowing it, we can accidentally crush their dreams. An example is when we truly believe in them and believe they can do anything but we feel obligated to direct them to the most viable and financially sound choice.

We are compelled to warn them because we actually believe that we can protect them from failure or heartbreak. We feel it is our responsibility to tell them that they will never be able to succeed in their unlikely venture. But dreamers perceive these responses as a statement about their talents and abilities. Discouraging a dream sends this underlying message: *"You don't have what it takes to succeed in that endeavor. Let someone more qualified live that dream. You should pick something less difficult and risky. You would be more successful doing something ordinary. You should be more practical."* Besides that, God is the only one that is able to protect our loved ones from failure and heartbreak. He is the only one that can and should be directing their steps! We should step over and let God be God in their lives.

So how should we react when a friend or family member wants to take a drastic step toward an improbable dream? How do we avoid contributing to a negative mind-set in a dreamer? Let me share with you how my husband and I responded to a recent idea our daughters brought to us.

We have three little girls. I love watching them and listening to them dream. They are full of joy. Sometimes, they have the wildest ideas. The current one is "Brush Bot." A Brush Bot is a toothbrush that you snap onto your teeth. It cleans your teeth, flosses, and to top that, it can spray breath freshener into your mouth when your breath is stinky.

I love the idea, but is it practical or realistic that my children could build this? Their goal is to build it by the end of the summer. As a mom, I have two options: I could list all the reasons why a Brush Bot wouldn't work and how difficult it would be to build, or I could encourage their dreaming and help them take the next step.

I chose to help them with the next step. Since we have zero knowledge in the field of inventing electronic devices, we helped our kids identify *only* the next step. We suggested that they draw a picture of the Brush Bot. After that was complete, we determined that the next step was to write down, in as much detail as possible, how the Brush Bot will work.

Guiding Your Children's Dreams

Learning to respond to your children's outrageous ideas with gentle guidance rather than caution and doubt takes intentional practice. We have plenty of opportunity to practice dream-nurturing responses in our home because our kids are big dreamers.

Instead of telling our daughters that their "big dream" would be impossible, my husband instructs them to journal their ideas. They pray and consider the details, draw pictures, and ask God to direct their steps, open doors, etc.

This is a great process because it teaches kids to process through the details and develop problem-solving skills. If siblings are working together, it also promotes a team environment and unity in the family.

Take the time to help your kids break down huge dreams into bite-sized pieces...your own imagination will benefit as well.

———

Rather than killing their dream with our own reasoning, we walked with them through the next steps. We are training them to pursue their dreams, to take risks, to live outside their comfort zone, to take initiative, to thoroughly consider their ideas, and to trust that God will plant His dreams in their heart.

More important, because we have invested time in pursuing their dreams hand in hand with them, our relationship with them is strengthened. As an added benefit, they learn to figure out how to take practical steps to reach their dreams without our direct input.

If you have unintentionally imposed a negative mind-set on someone's dream, or if you have abandoned your dreams because of other's pessimistic (often labeled "realistic") opinions, know that it is never too late to shake the cynical outlook and convert to a dream lifter.

My sister Kathleen remembered how to dream after many years of feeling lost with no ambition. She attended college only because she had been conditioned all her life to believe that was what she was supposed to do. She had been told that it was the only way to successfully support herself. She didn't know what she wanted to do. She assumed it was the next required step in life.

After she graduated from college, she still wasn't sure what to do with her life. She described herself as dreamless, passionless, and directionless. We invited her to begin dreaming again when she was with us one summer. In the process, she couldn't conceive a single dream. She shared with us that she had actually forgotten how to dream! She hadn't intentionally lost the ability, but over time, routine, people, and insecurity had eroded her dreams.

> **When we reason our own way out of obeying God, we value our own opinion more than we trust God.**

Throughout the summer, she opened up about the dreams that she had determined were ridiculous or impossible. Building a *Dreamwall* revealed that God had a specific purpose for her and that anything is possible! As Kathleen rekindled God's dreams within, she found that she loved music, writing, and singing! She began pursuing her dreams and which led to co-writing a song that same year along with the help of recording artist, Marcy Priest.

The root of a negative mind-set about your dreams is usually the desire to please other people. Man's opinion is often more valued than God's. When we reason our own way out of doing something that God has told us to do, we value our own discernment more than we trust God's commands.

But if we replace negative thoughts with God's truth, we can become filled with His dreams for us. When we partner with Him, He can achieve more than we could ever imagine. Trust that God's wisdom is higher than your own.

Let God be true, and every man a liar.

~ ROMANS 3:4

Chapter 4

SIGNS THAT YOU ARE STUCK

"One should be able to see things as hopeless and yet be determined to make them otherwise."

~ F. SCOTT FITZGERALD

Living in a state of fear and negativity may have you stuck. Your life may feel caught in a rut of hopelessness or complacency because of a tiresome and uninspiring routine, or maybe you feel obligated to be "responsible" and "practical." Words like can't, shouldn't, or won't are signs that reveal your dreaming ability has probably been imprisoned.

When I worked in public accounting, my clients would say that I was not a "typical" accountant. Today, I am certain I wasn't created to be an accountant. I chose that path because it seemed reasonable. I wish someone had seen in me all the signs that pointed to me taking the easy road –signs that I was losing hope in my dreams and getting stuck on the path of least resistance.

It is possible to identify someone who has lost hope. We are going to discuss a few of those signs.

First, what do people with hope look like? You can usually spot them a mile away—especially if you are hopeless. They might rub you the wrong way because they are spunky with tons of energy. They are hard workers who appear to work tirelessly. Their mission is urgent in their mind and they passionately draw others to their cause. They build others up and are constantly in search of good people to share in the vision and work.

We had the opportunity to mentor a man we will call Zach, who had played a significant role in organized crime. His life had been changed by the redemptive work of Jesus Christ. He was on a fast and furious mission to disciple struggling teens and others he knew were heading down the same path of life he had chosen. Because Zach could talk the talk, he was able to gain tremendous influence with these men. The change in Zach's life motivated others to hear what he had to say about Jesus and to learn God's word from him. He was tirelessly driven to serve these young men. Faced with the constant threat of significant danger, Zach radiated hope that was contagious.

Those who have lost hope are usually easy to spot. Let's look at a few common characteristics of people who are stuck in a negative mind-set.

They lack motivation—Their lack of motivation and enthusiasm is evident in their daily actions. It's the person who is always late to work, watches the clock all day, and sneaks out early. When operating outside your God-given calling, dedication to work does not endure. Exhaustion and burn out are imminent.

They give minimum effort—People who have lost hope have no passion for what they do. They are content simply to maintain the minimum requirement without looking for opportunities to do more. With no sense of importance or urgency, their daily activities become a means to an end rather than a way to contribute something meaningful or valuable to this world.

They are critical of others—Another indication that someone is losing hope and has given up on his or her dreams is consistent criticism of others. When you have lost hope and feel terrible about your own life, pointing out flaws in others somehow makes you feel better about yourself. If you recognize that someone you know is constantly criticizing others, it may be a sign that he or she is losing hope in life and no longer pursuing God-given dreams.

They play the joker—Many people who have lost hope cover up their lack of direction and ambition with sarcastic jokes or self-deprecating comments. They have learned, probably at a young age, to protect their pride by making fun of themselves before someone else can hurt them. Were you one of those kids who always talked themselves down? I still do it today. I'll point out, "Oh, I have gained weight." I do this before anyone can notice that my cheerleader body is not what it used to be. *Why* would I do this? I do it because I have condemned myself to failure. I'm actually sending the message that I have given up hope in myself.

Do you know someone who always jokingly ridicules or speaks negatively about his or her own characteristics or abilities? This can be a sign of someone who has lost hope. Constant self-deprecating humor can be an indicator of a lack of self-value. Jokers have lost touch with their dreams and God's call on their lives. They are insecure, but working hard to ensure no one knows it. But I'll let you in on a little secret. We know.

They are quitters—Those who are losing hope will often show a pattern of quitting in their lives. I grew up in a very critical home. Almost daily, I heard about all the things that I didn't do well! I can hardly remember an encouraging word. I was starved for encouragement and would search anywhere to find it. I joined teams that built me up. I fell in love with any boy interested in me. But as soon as anything negative was spoken, I would bail. Quit. Leave. Run! Because of my home life, I could not bear outside criticism. I spent over half of my life running anytime the going got rough! I quit on anything and anyone I assumed would let me down. I never could have fulfilled God's call on my life with those insecurities looming over me! I lost my hope. Are you a runner? I am confident you know one. If you know someone who is a runner, chances are, he or she has lost hope too.

Perhaps the signs of losing hope are evident in your life. Maybe you don't relate to any of these, but you feel hopeless because you have been defeated in the area of finances, have strained relationships, or have overwhelming responsibilities.

If you are stuck in a hopeless place, it's time to turn it around! Are you ready to take your hope back? Start by finding something to be thankful for, no matter what your circumstances are! I lost my mom when I was thirty-seven years old. Oh, wow, did I hurt! My heart ached daily. I could have easily lost my hope, but I chose to find something that I could thank God for. When I considered a friend who had lost her mother at age twelve, I immediately began to praise God for the years I had my mom! The more I contemplated all my blessings, the more my joy returned!

> Application: Write down a list of one hundred things that you are thankful for.

No matter how dismal your life may feel; I believe you can find at least one hundred good things in your life. You may be surprised at how long your gratitude list grows.

My family attended a camp together where one day we studied water creatures. We used nets to trap all sorts of strange-looking animals and insects in a small, but active, stream. As we wrapped up, the guide asked, "How could you tell this was a healthy water source?" The answer was obvious. The river was breeding all sorts of life in and around its water and shores. People who are alive with hope are living life and creating life all around them. I know you are alive in Christ, and I know you hunger for this life for yourself.

If you still have breath in you, God still has a purpose for you! Encourage hope in yourself! If you don't stir yourself up, you will settle to the bottom. It is easier to follow the easy path, but it's stagnant. There is no life in a stagnant pond.

Delight yourself in the Lord, and he will give you the desires of your heart.

~ PSALM 37:4

Chapter 5

BEYOND A LIMITED LIFE

"Beware in your prayers, above everything else, of limiting God, not only by unbelief, but by fancying that you know what He can do."

~ ANDREW MURRAY

You can be a dream killer even if you are someone who has goals and aspirations. You may not be stuck in fear, negativity, or hopelessness, but if you are not in tune with God, your worldly ambitions could be killing God's dreams for you. Your goals may be admirable and well-intentioned, but if they are not born out of your God-given imagination, they can stand in the way of God's plan. You can actually limit God's ability to reveal and fulfill his bigger dreams for you when your attention is not on Him.

God Himself cannot be limited. His purposes will be carried out. However, the extent to which you are used in those plans is up to your willingness to surrender your will to God's way.

Romans 1:21 (NASB) says, *"For even though they knew God, they did not honor Him as God or give thanks, but they became futile in their speculations, and their foolish heart was darkened."*

When you stop glorifying God and giving thanks to Him, your mind and imagination become focused on selfish and worldly ambitions. But God designed you to be all about Him, not all about you. He desires to have our imaginations and our dreams so he can work through us for His glory!

> **You can be a dream killer even if you are someone who has goals and aspirations.**

It's time to do a heart check. Is your mind turned to God with a thankful attitude? Or are the things of this world overtaking your mind and imagination? Don't let your heart be darkened. Don't allow your mind-set to limit God.

Let's look more closely at the downward spiral of God's people in Romans 1:21.

DIDN'T GLORIFY GOD

VAIN THOUGHTS AND IMAGINATION

UNGRATEFUL

HARD HEART

They didn't recognize God.

This verse says they knew God but gave Him no glory. This means that they gave God no distinction. They did not recognize God as their source of life, health, or prosperity. They did not admire God as absolutely magnificent. Their life was in a rut. In their eyes, God had become common and familiar.

For the first time ever, we have an NBA professional basketball franchise in our home city. Our team is magnificent. Today, they are famed and highly regarded. Whether they win or lose, our fans are known as some of the most faithful in the league. Next year, or ten years from now, this could change. Once familiarity sets in, our community's support might transition from unconditional to performance-based. Today, we are all excited to have the team.

The people described in Romans came to expect God's provision. Because they became comfortable and familiar with God's miracles, they gave Him no glory. This is ridiculous, but I can almost understand how this happened. For the past two years, my family has experienced the power of God operate in almost unimaginable ways. It's easy to become so accustomed to walking in His power that I overlook a miracle. How is that possible? Familiarity.

Is your life in a rut? Has God become familiar to you? Or do you live each day glorifying our magnificent God?

> **Familiarity and comfort with God can cause us to overlook miracles in our lives.**

They gave no thanks.

It is very easy to take for granted things that are familiar. When a new business earns its first dollar, it is framed and mounted on the wall. Three years later, God is still providing for the owner, and the business is still successful, but the dollars become expected.

We celebrate our initial successes, but once familiarity sets in, we rarely celebrate. In Romans 1:21, the Romans become familiar with God and, therefore, stop giving thanks to Him as their provider. A grateful heart teaches you not to take God's blessings for granted and view all circumstances (good or terrible) through the eyes of our all-powerful God!

Magnify God with a thankful heart! Learn to look for miracles in your life. At a minimum, you can be thankful that Christ lived the life you should have lived and paid the price you should have paid.

Speculation took over imaginations.

Intelligence is highly regarded in our society. Most people with power and influence are automatically attributed the highest ranks of intelligence, and we are trained to value reasoning and intellect. However, our intelligence is futile outside of God's wisdom.

In this scripture, the people's analytical decision making became ineffective because it was not guided by God's wisdom. I can only imagine the chaos and confusion of a group of people completely without God's wisdom.

Are you confused? Is your life chaotic? Are you worn out with analyzing your situation or your purpose? Have you elevated your opinions, imagination, plans, and logic above God's word?

> **Intelligence is futile outside of God's wisdom.**

Their hearts darkened.

As a young man, my husband worked on farms and ranches. Along with many other boys his age, he hauled hay each summer. They gathered hay bales from the field, stacked them on a truck, and moved them to a barn. By the end of the summer, these boys' hands were thickly callused from those months of abuse.

His hands wouldn't have been callused if he had only worked one day or one week. Our hearts can become darkened in a similar way. Just as it takes time to build up a callus on your hands, a hardened heart is the result of long-term abuse.

The people described in Romans no longer recognized God or gave thanks; they became speculative and stopped pursuing God's wisdom. Over time, they surrendered to their selfish desires. As a result, their hearts became callused to God.

Where are you? Is your heart hardened and callused toward God? If so, all of your dreams and ambitions will be misdirected, guided by your own thoughts and not the imagination that God has given you. Give your desires to God. Simply pray and ask God to flood the eyes of your heart with a deep and intimate understanding of who He is and who you are in Him. Renew your mind with God's truth. Read it as a love letter written directly to you and for you. Allow God to reveal any place in your heart that is callused so He can replace it with His truth.

Maybe you realize that you are living in the downward spiral and have limited God's dreams for you. Are you ready to turn back? The cool thing about our God is that He is always ready to restore you! The solution to turning back to our wonderful God, simply flip Romans 1:21 around:

- Start glorifying God.
- Give God thanks.
- Use your imagination to consider what *God can* do.

Your hard and darkened heart will be softened, and your goals, ambitions, and dreams will not be in vain— God will inspire your dreams!

Noah was a hero in faith. In Hebrews 11, his heart was sensitive toward God. Why else would he agree to build an ark? Why would he have sacrificed 120 years of his life to prepare for a flood when it had never rained before? His actions were not logical. Noah was someone who was in tune with God. Noah had to have his mind and imagination laser-focused on God. His focus enabled him to hear, visualize, and carry out God's dreams for him.

Are you ready to lose any hardness in your heart and turn it into a soft, hearing one that is sensitive to God?

Begin by praising God at all times and focusing your imagination and mind on Him! When you do this, He will place His dreams for you in your heart and you will not be able to contain them!

I tell you the truth, if you have faith as small as a mustard seed, you can say to this mountain, 'Move from here to there and it will move.' Nothing will be impossible for you.

~ MATTHEW 17:20

Part 2

TAKING YOUR HOPE BACK

Chapter 6

IDENTITY RULES—LIES DROOL

"When God looks at you, he doesn't see you;
he sees the One who surrounds you. That means
that failure is not a concern for you. Your
victory is secure."

~ MAX LUCADO

What is your opinion of yourself? How you view yourself will determine your ability to accomplish all that God has for you.

The Israelites saw themselves as small, weak, and incapable of conquering the men residing in the Promised Land because they perceived them as giants. You can read about this in Numbers 13.

If you believe you are a weak, barely saved sinner, then you may back down when life gets tough. It will get tough. Plowing new ground requires hard work, perseverance, and a steady trust in the Lord.

If you view yourself through God's eyes—a forgiven, chosen, loved, blameless, saint who is filled to the full with the Holy Spirit—then when things get hard, you will not back down because you know you are a servant of Christ! You are confident that in everything you do, you represent the One True God. You know that where He guides, He provides. So when the provision isn't present, you know and trust that it is coming.

It is critical that you know your identity in Jesus Christ! It is the beginning or the end.

If we are going to defeat negativity, fear, and distractions to reclaim our hope, we must start by knowing our true identity in Christ.

When I was three years old, my alcoholic dad abandoned our family. At that young age, I assumed, *What is wrong with me that caused my daddy to leave me? Am I unlovable?* I struggled to understand. I didn't realize this at the time, but this event deeply rooted a lie in me: I am unlovable and not wanted.

My dad did not intend to cause me to feel unloved or unwanted, but it was my perception.

> **Anything that you believe to be true will impact your life as if it were true, although it's a lie!**

When I was ten years old, my life took a turn for the worse. For four years, I was molested in my own home. I cannot properly convey the kind of damage this abuse does in a child. If you have been hurt similarly to me, then you know how devastating it is to have your body used for something it wasn't designed for.

I felt shame.

I was confused.

I wasn't safe in my home.

The abuse didn't stop there. Abusers need to have control over you. They will demean you to keep you quiet. Therefore, the mental abuse began. I was called "stupid," "idiot," "brat," and many others that I have worked hard to forget. Although I am a smart and capable person, I believed I was unintelligent for many years—into my late twenties.

I worked hard to achieve things because I was trying to prove to everyone (including myself) that I wasn't dumb! I graduated college with a degree in accounting, became a certified public accountant and was hired by one of the top accounting firms in the nation. I eventually became a manager in my firm—a position that requires skillful management of a heavy workload and many challenges.

Because the lie I bought was deeply embedded in my heart, every time I made a mistake or a client was dissatisfied, I would crumble. I vacillated between feelings of hope and feelings of despair. One day I was at the top of my game. The next I felt lower than the dirt— under everyone's feet. I lived on a roller coaster of people's opinions and perspectives. Albert Einstein stated, *"Everybody is a genius. But if you judge a fish by its ability to climb a tree, it will live its whole life believing that it is stupid."*

> **It's virtually impossible to complete the calling on your life when you base your identity on what others say about you and the lies you believe about yourself.**

To feel loved, I shamelessly searched for someone to meet my need. Oh, the grief in my life over so many failed relationships. I tirelessly pursued anyone who would deem me as someone worthy of love and who would not reject me. What I didn't know is that the huge gap in my heart would never be filled through another person! All my efforts actually prevented my escape to freedom.

Lies believed can inhibit God's powerful plan for our lives. The biggest deception preventing me from achieving my dreams was insecurity. My self-doubts and self-deprecation were rooted in the false beliefs I had heard and also the negative words I concluded about myself as a young girl:

IDENTITY TRASH

INSECURE	DRY	LAST
INVISIBLE	JEALOUS	UNQUALIFIED
WOUNDED	SHAME	DIRTY
FEARFUL	ANXIETY	REJECTED
UNSTABLE	POOR BODY IMAGE	TRAPPED
UNWORTHY	GUILTY	INSIGNIFICANT
TIRED	GRIEVED	DEPRESSED
RESENTFUL	BITTER	ENVIOUS
PRIDEFUL	MEAN	EMPTY
NEEDY	POWER TRIP	LOST
LAZY	OVER WORKED	OVER WHELMED
LONELY	SICK	PEOPLE PLEASER
SUICIDAL	POWERLESS	ABUSED
ADDICTED	CHILDLESS	SINGLE
WORRY	FINANCES	STARTING OVER
WIDOWED	DIVIDED	ANGRY

"You are so stupid!"
"You are dirty!"
"You are shameful."
"You are unloved."
"You are unworthy."
"Everyone will eventually abandon you."
"You are ugly."

Everything that I had believed about myself was a lie. When I finally realized this, it opened up a whole can of worms! Now I didn't know who I was. If I wasn't all of those things, who was I?

It's virtually impossible to complete the calling on your life when you base your identity on what others say about you and the lies you believe about yourself.

To release God's dreams from within me, I literally had to smash everything I believed about *who* I was and start over! Another ragamuffin soul like myself, Brennan Manning, has shared this wisdom: *"Real freedom is freedom from the opinions of others. Above all, freedom from your opinions about yourself."*

People frequently ask me, "How did you change from such a broken, insecure, needy person?" They didn't see the process of my change. They see the person I am today: *healed* and walking in total freedom! They desire to be restored, too. They hunger for *freedom* too!

However, they didn't observe the many hours of hard work—the times when I was alone battling to know myself in this new identity! They didn't witness the years of blood, sweat, and tears while I fought for this freedom! They didn't observe the many hours I poured over the Bible searching for truth for up to five hours a day! They didn't know the desperately starving, furiously pursuing woman who wasn't willing to tolerate another day of being lied to!

They long for the results, but they usually aren't willing to do the hard work to get them! They usually aren't fed up enough with the trash they have believed!

"Stop determining your worth and value by what other people say. Be determined by what the Word of God says."
~ JOYCE MEYER

———

Once you have decided that you are ready to trash the lies and believe what God says about you, you must do the hardest thing of all: stop trying to protect yourself. The instinct for self-preservation will cause you to try to hide the broken parts of yourself rather than giving your brokenness to God to mend.

Because I was wounded emotionally and spiritually at a very early age, I lived most of my life broken and full of sin and pain. I had fallen into such deep sin that the shame and guilt wrecked me. My need to be loved led me to search out love and acceptance in all the wrong places.

When I first surrendered to Jesus, I spent all my time trying to help God rebuild my life. I tried to use my own resources to restore all the pieces to become a whole person again. But I was mistaken. I thought I had started life whole, then became flawed. So I was determined to be whole again!

IDENTITY TRUTHS		
ACCEPTED	COMPLETE	ALIVE
BLAMELESS	WISDOM	NEVER REJECTED
INDWELT	RIGHTEOUS	FREE
FRIEND	CHOSEN	LOVED
FORGIVEN	NEW	SPECIAL
CLEAN	SHELTERED	HEALED
MASTERPIECE	RESTED	STABLE
SECURE	COMFORTED	FATHERED
DAILY BREAD	PROVIDER	PROTECTED
SEALED	BELONG TO JESUS	IN HARMONY
REDEEMED	DELIVERED	SAVED
HOLY SPIRIT	AUTHORITY	UNDISTURBED
UNMERITED FAVOR	ADOPTED	PLEASING
HIDDEN IN CHRIST	UNITED	SET APART
VICTORIOUS	CO-HEIR WITH JESUS	BEAUTIFUL
PRECIOUS	CALLED	RESTORED

But God revealed to me, *"You know, Sheri, you didn't start off as a whole person. You were always incomplete without Me."* I had always been broken; it wasn't until I surrendered to God that He made me whole! I worked for years to do what only God could do in a moment! If you are broken, you are in good company. All of us are flawed and fall short of God's best. This verse gave me an "aha" moment!

All have sinned and fall short of the glory of God
(ROMANS 3:23).

You are special because God molded you, and God doesn't create mistakes! You aren't loved because you are loveable. You are loved because God is love. You aren't valued because you're valuable. You're valuable because God made you. If you have been broken, I hope this verse encourages you that God wants to restore you completely, too!

Therefore, if anyone is in Christ, he is a new creation; the old has gone, the new has come
(2 CORINTHIANS 5:17)!

I really love this verse because it gives me indescribable peace to know that, as broken as I was, God still pulled all the pieces of my life together and restored me. The scars are gone!

When we live out of a broken, incomplete view of ourselves, we are fragile and hopeless. In this state, we will never be able to believe the amazing dreams God has for us. If we are nursing our tender wounds, God cannot fill us with His hope and vision for our lives.

Are you ready to be set free and start down the path to carrying out God's dreams for your life? Are you willing to invest pure effort into gaining something really awesome? FREEDOM baby!

Start today—decide that you are no longer willing to be defined by what has been done to you, what has been spoken about you, or what you have done.

The only thing that's true about you is what God says about you. Romans 3:4 says, *"Let God be true and every man a liar."* To let God be true, you have to know what He says about you. Maybe at this point you realize you may not know God personally yet. If you hunger to know Him, flip to the *Living the Dream* section at the end of this book to find out how!

> **We have to know *who* we are in Christ! Our identity isn't in what we do, others opinions, what's been done to us, or even the accusations of our inner voice! We are who God says we are, period!**

So who does God say you are? Below I have listed a few of the powerful truths God says about you. I review this list often myself. When you read these, say them aloud or read them in the mirror to yourself. If it's hard for you to believe, then do it every day until you know it in your soul!

- You are blessed in the heavenly realms with every spiritual blessing in Christ (Ephesians 1:3).
- He chose you in Him before the creation of the world (Ephesians 1:4).
- You are holy and blameless in His sight (Ephesians 1:4).
- In His love, He predestined you to be adopted through Jesus Christ (Ephesians 1:5).

- He has freely given you His grace (Ephesians 1:6).
- You have redemption in Him through Christ (Ephesians 1:7).
- You are forgiven (Ephesians 1:7).
- He has made known the mystery of His will to you (Ephesians 1:9).
- You are chosen and have been predestined according to His plan (Ephesians 1:11).
- You were included in Christ when you heard the word of truth, the gospel of your salvation. When you believed, you were marked with a seal, the promised Holy Spirit, who is a deposit guaranteeing your inheritance (Ephesians 1:14–15).
- God has great love for you (Ephesians 2:4).
- You have been saved by His grace (Ephesians 2:5).
- You have been saved by grace, through faith— and this not from yourself; it is the gift of God— not by works (Ephesians 2:8–9).
- You are God's masterpiece (Ephesians 2:10 NLT).

Isn't it amazing how much you are loved and valued by God? When you know this truth, others' opinions pale in comparison to God's! Learn to view yourself and others through God's eyes, and you will never be the same!

If you find it difficult to accept the things that God says about you, then you need to spend time getting to know God more intimately. We will dig deeper into this

in the next chapter. It's in knowing and trusting God
that the verses above will bring you so much security
and confidence!

Remember the story of David and Goliath? Perhaps
you heard about this story when you were young or
maybe you have never heard it. Either way, we are going
to look at it through a new lens.

David faced many criticisms from his brother, the
king, and Goliath, yet he still had the courage to face the
obstacles in front of him! He was willing to face a literal
giant, against all odds, because he knew who he was
in Christ! David knew
he was God's chosen
child. He was secure
in his Father and his
identity—so secure,
that no one's com-
ments could shake his
resolve. This should
be our goal as believ-
ers. We should know
God and our identity through His eyes so well that we
run toward our giants with great faith like David in 1
Samuel.

> **With confidence
> in God we can
> run toward
> giants with
> great faith.**

The world shows love and encouragement based on performance. When you are succeeding by the world's standards, the world will love you. When you are not measuring up, you get a big, fat helping of discouragement. If you hope to be a wishy-washy Christian whose faith ebbs and flows based on people, then form your identity by the world's reaction to you. But if you desire to have the confidence and courage to reach for God-sized dreams, you must truly know your identity in Christ.

Keep your mind on God's view of you. He loves you. It will change your journey!

Before I formed you in the womb I knew you, before you were born I set you apart; I appointed you as a prophet to the nations.

~ JEREMIAH 1:5

Chapter 7

WHO CAN YOU TRUST

"Never be afraid to trust an unknown future to a known God."

~ CORRIE TEN BOOM

It will be difficult to stick with God's view of you if you have not learned to fully trust Him. However, if you spend much time with Him at all, you will discover that your Heavenly Father is the most trustworthy aspect of your life. When you have an intimate relationship with Him, you will know for yourself that your God loves you deeply and He will never leave you or forsake you.

We trust in what we know.

It's in knowing God well that we trust His words. When we trust Him more than anyone else in the world, no one else's opinions or criticisms matter! We don't depend on others for our value. When you know God intimately, you obtain His counsel first and trust it most! A close relationship with Christ is what enables you to really trust that your identity in Him is secure and *true*!

The same is true with any relationship. The better you know someone, the more you are able to trust in that person (as long as he or she proves to be —trustworthy). As you learn more about a person's character and witness that character in action, trust is built Ωnaturally.

God longs for you to know Him well. He has pursued a relationship with mankind since the creation of the world. He is inviting you to get to know Him better and let Him show you that He is trustworthy. Believe Him. The extensive list of things He calls you are true. He desires you to pursue the dreams that He has planted in your heart.

David knew His God intimately. You can read more about David in 1 Samuel. I imagine David singing praises to His God while in the shepherd's field. I believe He and God talked as best friends. David's intimate trust in God gave him great courage to pursue God's goals for him, including facing an actual giant! And we have a greater covenant with God than David did, because as followers of Christ, the Holy Spirit lives in us. If we believe in God's identity for us, the Holy Spirit fills, guides, and teaches us.

Farris Family Story

"Being totally debt free was one of the dreams on our *Stickie Dreamwall*. We believed God would provide. Shortly after, we received an unexpected $2,000. I also received an unexpected $500 Christmas bonus, as well as a pay raise! We are on track to be completely debt free, except for our home, before the end of the year!"

> **God can do amazing things when you place your trust in Him.**

Knowing a person and knowing about him or her are two different things. I know a few things *about* the president of the United States, but if I ran up to him to say, "Hi," he would probably give me a confused look...right before I was detained by the Secret Service! I could not hang out with him or trust him with the most personal areas of my life, because I don't *know* him. There is a huge difference between knowing about someone and really knowing that person—having a true relationship with him or her.

> *Not everyone who says to me,*
> *'Lord, Lord,' will enter the kingdom*
> *of heaven, but only he who does the will*
> *of my Father who is in heaven. Many*
> *will say to me on that day, 'Lord, Lord,*
> *did we not prophesy in your name, and*
> *in your name drive out demons and*
> *perform many miracles?' Then I will tell*
> *them plainly, 'I never knew you. Away*
> *from me, you evildoers'*
> (MATTHEW 7:21–23).

Clearly, knowing God is what life is all about! John 17:3 reads, eternal life is knowing God. It's not only a destination—heaven. It's about knowing God—here *and* there! How well do you know your God?

Maybe you have been hurt, and it made you angry with God. Or maybe you have a misunderstanding of who God is because you never really sought Him on your own. Maybe you assume your sins are too awful to be forgiven and this leaves you unlovable. Believe me, I understand.

It took me a long time to be able to trust God with the details of my life. I used to worry all the time. Seriously, I was anxious *all* the time about war, money, dying in a plane or car accident, people's opinions of me, etc. The list was unending. I had a relationship with God, but I didn't truly know Him and because of this, I struggled to place my absolute trust in Him. I could not force myself to do it. I wasn't sure if God was trustworthy. Was he really for me? Would He strike me down with a disease? Looking back, I realize it was crazy. I am such a peaceful person now. I don't worry—well, almost never. Sure, when we had a huge earthquake in the middle of my tornado state, I was a little rattled, but because I *know* my God, I immediately placed my trust in Him. Over the years, as I read the Bible and came to know God—truly know how good He is to His children—I was overwhelmed at how much I had misunderstood Him in the past.

It's in truly getting to know God for ourselves—through our own relationship with Him—that we are able to stand firm trusting Him, even in the worst circumstances, because we know with full confidence that He's got our back!

God is calling you. He loves you so much! He is waiting on you so He can love on you!

Know God More Intimately

So, how do you get to know God? Keep it simple. It's similar to getting to know a new friend. How would you get to know someone? You would ask questions, share stories, and spend time together.

God is not your typical friend—He is never too busy for you. Talk to Him; He answers anytime you call on Him. You can set aside a specific time each day to talk with Him, but my favorite way to communicate with God is to continue the conversation with Him all day long. If I could call God on my phone, it would be as if He's waiting on the speakerphone all day. He's available to chat throughout the day.

You might be questioning, *Sure, I talk to God, but how do I hear back from Him*?

God made it so easy to hear and know Him. How? The Bible. He gave us stories, descriptions of His character, promises, and encouragement that reveal who He is and why He deserves our trust. The Bible is true, active, alive, powerful, and full of awesomeness about *who* God is.

> **God is not your typical friend. He is never too busy for you.**

Knowing and trusting God are the true treasures. A relationship with Him is far more important than anything! It's in Him that our heart's desires are fulfilled! *Delight yourself in the LORD and he will give you the desires of your heart* (Psalm 37:4). Pursue a relationship with God as if your life depends on it, because hope results from intimacy with God. Without hope, dreams die.

If you need help in knowing *how* to know God more intimately, check out our free Bible study at www.soarwithgod.com. The "Seek" part of the study focuses on knowing and falling in love with God.

I keep asking that the God of our Lord Jesus Christ, the glorious Father, may give you the Spirit of wisdom and revelation, so that you may know him better.

~ EPHESIANS 1:17

But they also fearfully proclaimed that the walls of the city towered as high as the sky and *"We look like grasshoppers in comparison to how big they are"* (Numbers 13:33 *paraphrased*).

These men inspected and then over exaggerated the obstacles. Common sense says that walls aren't built to reach the sky. That's ridiculous. But their fearful *imaginations* magnified everything they witnessed. As they considered the land, they mostly saw impossibilities which filled them with fear and hesitation.

> **The mind is a powerful tool that will either lead you toward your dreams or away from them.**

As word began to spread throughout the community, people became too afraid to charge in and take God's substantial gift. Deuteronomy 1:21 reads, *"See, the Lord your God has given you the land. Go up and take possession of it as the Lord, the God of your fathers, told you. Do not be afraid; do not be discouraged."* Although the Lord had already given them the victory, they chose fear over faith and did not trust His promises. They chose to return to the wilderness rather than seize God's dreams for them.

Something may seem impossible, but God wants his children to use their imaginations to conceive what He can do in the unseen. Check out what Ephesians 3:20 says, "*Now to him who is able to do immeasurably more than all we ask or imagine, according to his power that is at work within us.*" In other versions, it says, "*more than we can dream or hope.*"

Artist-architect John Hench, who worked on Disney-land from its beginning (and on Disney films for fifteen years before that), recalls when he first heard about the possibility of a Disney amusement park: "It was back in the forties. I lived on Riverside Drive in Burbank, quite near the Studio. I remember several Sundays seeing Walt across the street in a weed-filled lot, standing, visualizing, all by himself. I remember one feature was going to be a singing waterfall, just one of several ideas. But the longer Walt thought about the park, the more ideas he got, and suddenly the weed-filled lot wasn't big enough."

> **Something may appear impossible to you, but with God all things are possible.**

Disney's imagination led him to create the "Happiest Place on Earth." The Israelites' imagination led them back into the wilderness for forty years. They chose the wilderness over the Land of Milk and Honey because in their minds they magnified the obstacles in front of them. Your imagination will always lead you somewhere. It will lead you into the wilderness, or it'll lead you into God's Promised Land.

Where do you aspire to be? I hope you responded, "The Promised Land." If that is where you aim to arrive, you'll need to tame the menacing part of your mind that fills your head with doubts and surrender your imagination to God. Awaken your imagination to the power of God in the next chapter. Ready for the journey? Read on, my friend.

Jesus replied, "What is impossible with man is possible with God."

~ LUKE 18:27

Chapter 9

SURRENDER YOUR IMAGINATION

*"The Christian is the one whose imagination
should fly beyond the stars."*

~ FRANCIS A. SCHAEFFER

Your God-given imagination is creative, ambitious, loving, and compassionate. Your God-given dreams are inspiring, motivating, and exciting. In fact, your imagination is only being used in the way it was designed when it is surrendered to inspiration from God.

Hebrews 11:1 says, *"Now faith is being sure of what we hope for and certain of what we do not see."* When

To become God-sized dreamers, we must reclaim our hope!

you compare that definition of faith to the definition of imagination, which is "forming mental images of things not present to the senses," notice they are very similar. You might even say that our imaginations are built on faith. *Your positive imagination is where hope is conceived!*

So if we are going to take our hope back so that we can become dreamers of God-sized dreams, we have to surrender our imaginations to God in the same way we surrender our lives to Him in faith when we become followers of Christ.

Is your imagination surrendered to God, or is it still working against you, leading you into the wilderness? He wants your imagination to be inspired by Him.

The Bible says God *can do more than we can think, ask, or imagine* (Ephesians 3:20 *paraphrased*). But whether you realize it or not, your imagination can become suppressed when you're only focused on the giants and huge obstacles you face. When you're focused on the worst-case scenarios and the what-ifs, that is your imagination working against you.

> **Hope is conceived in your positive imagination!**

What if instead of allowing our minds to automatically cross into negativity, we led them immediately to focus on Jesus: *"This difficulty is no big deal for Jesus. He has raised people from the dead, and He can also take care of this problem!"* God teaches His children how to keep their minds constantly on Him and His wonders instead of life's worries and pains. *You will keep him in perfect peace, whose mind is stayed on You, because he trusts in You* (Isaiah 26:3 (NKJV)). When we trust in Him, we have His peace.

Because I keep my mind on what God did today, yesterday, and every day, it captures my runaway mind so that my imagination aligns with God's dreams for me. We must reject any thought that disagrees with God's Word and continue to replace the trash with Truth!

Casting down imaginations and every high thing that exalteth itself against the knowledge of God, and bringing into captivity every thought to the obedience of Christ

(2 CORINTHIANS 10:5 (KJV)).

Our family developed a game called *Truth or Trash* (the App is available for download in the iTunes store) that has become a fundamental part of how we view life. We teach our kids to separate the truth from the lies, and the game teaches discernment and starts deep conversations. If anyone in our family speaks something that is untrue, someone else will immediately identify it, "Capture that; that's trash." We need to be alert and on our toes. This game is great practice.

It's remarkable how many times a day we say things that are not true without realizing it. Have you ever caught yourself saying, "That will never work," before you've even give yourself a chance to succeed with a new idea? How many times have you dismissed a genuine compliment from a friend with the assumption, *Oh, she's just being polite*? You must learn to capture that trash and take captive every thought that does not agree with God's truth.

If negativity creeps in your mind, cast it down and replace it with truth. For example, if you think, *I am stupid,* cast it down and contradict it, "No! I have the mind of Christ, and it doesn't matter if the world assumes I'm stupid." When you notice your negative attitude, sit down right away and write one hundred things you are thankful for. Remember the good things God has done in your life and the gifts He has blessed you with. Every time. If you do it enough, you will change. You will transform into a more positive person.

Coy's Story

Coy was once a stand-up comedian in Bakersfield, California, and is now a homeschooling mom in Oklahoma. She attended a *Stickie Dreamwall* session and was hit with the reality that she was a dream killer to her husband. She also realized that she had suppressed her own dreams and allowed her God-given imagination to become inactive.

Coy drove home with her mind spinning. *What would I say to my husband? How should I tell him my realization that I had killed his dreams? Was there too much damage to repair?*

But, much to her surprise, her husband turned it around on her. He inquired, "What dreams have you suppressed?"

She quickly spilled her deeply suppressed heart's desire to be a stand-up comedian again. One year to the date, she shared a Christian stand-up comedy act at the *very* same event where her dreams were awakened the year before.

Coy assumed that being a mom meant giving up those dreams. When you stop imagining yourself being successful at the things God has called you to, your dreams die. Your heart gives up hope, and it becomes easy to settle into a familiar daily routine.

—–

Don't stop asking God what He has planned for you. It may be to raise your children, start a new business, share Christ at work, teach a class, share your testimony, or write a book. Whatever it is, don't allow your imagination to become stagnant and unmoved by the things of God. Albert Einstein declared, *"Imagination is everything. It is the preview of life's coming attractions."* Open your heart and mind to discover the wonderful things God has in store for you.

Shift your focus, and cling to the promises of God. He tells us, *"And I will do whatever you ask in my name"* (John 14:13); *"Then the Lord your God will make you most prosperous in all the work of your hands"* (Deuteronomy 30:9); and *"But seek first his kingdom and his righteousness and all these things will be given to you as well"* (Matthew 6:33). God's promises are true. Focus on what God can do. He will take care of you if you allow Him to work through your life.

It's your choice. Today, choose to surrender your imagination to God, and get ready to experience powerful miracles!

Now faith is the substance of things hoped for, the evidence of things not seen.

~ HEBREWS 11:1 KJV

Chapter 10

THE HOPE RESCUE

"I'm telling you, unless you have a deliberate plan to encourage yourself in the Lord, you aren't going to be encouraged."

~ ANDREW WOMMACK

Now that you know who God says you are, how much He loves you, and how to overcome your defeatist imagination and surrender your mind to God, it's time to take your hope back!

I use the acronym **WWW.DO** to encourage myself in the Lord. The letters represent the phrase: *"When you know* **Who** *God is,* **Who** *you are, and* **What** *you have in Christ, you'll know what to* **do***."*

Who is God to you? Is He angry and ready to pounce on you every time you do something wrong? Or is He the God that is love, grace, and mercy? The way you view God will determine how you will stand in hard times. If you believe God is mad, you may believe that you deserve His punishment when you mess up. However, if you believe God is love and forgiveness, you will stand firm in His love no matter what comes your way. You will know that your God has your back!

If you are a believer in Christ, then you belong to God, the King of Kings. You are adopted into His family, and you will always be His child. Ephesians says it this way: *For he chose us in him before the creation of the world to be holy and blameless in his sight. In love he predestined us to be adopted as his sons through Jesus Christ, in accordance with his pleasure and will—to the praise of his glorious grace, which he has freely given us in the One he loves* (Ephesians 1:4–6). Adopted. Do you get that? That's a big deal! Adopted into the family of God.

The *Webster's Unabridged Dictionary* defines the word *adopt* as "to choose or take as one's own." If a family adopts a child, does that child belong to the family? Of course! Does he have any fewer privileges than the children born into the family? Heavens no. Who cares for the adopted child? The adoptive parents, not the biological mom or dad. Now, here is

> **When you know *who* you are in Christ, you have the ability to live continuously in God's power.**

an even better question. How will the adopted child know the adoptive parents love him? As he spends time with them, he will experience their love. The same is true with God. The more time you spend with Him in prayer and in His word, the more you will know the One *you belong to.*

Who are you? Remember, in chapter 6 we learned who we are in Christ. Let's review. Often we trust in who others think we are rather than what God says. In this life, how much time do we spend trying to "find" ourselves? We search for our true identity in the things we enjoy, family, careers, hobbies, etc. Something we do or something someone did to us can label us. Labels identify us with who others think we are. It's difficult because, unfortunately, words are sticky. Words from bosses, friends, family, and people can define us and stick to us in one moment…if we let them.

The truth is that once you are adopted into the kingdom of God, you become God's child. Only what God says about you is true. Period! All of the opinions, emotions, and actions that once defined you are forever eliminated—terminated. Through renewing your mind with truth and time spent with your adopted Father, in time, your mind will be convinced that what He says about you is true.

What do you have in Christ? When you are born again, you know that you are saved and have eternal life with God because of your salvation. Well, in the same way, you also have been given the Holy

Spirit. This means that the same power that raised Christ from the dead lives in you. You aren't just an average person who walks around hopeless and powerless, because you have God's power living in and for you!

Let's imagine that a royal family adopts a child. Their words have power and authority throughout the whole kingdom. Now what rights and privileges does the adopted child have? How will he know *what* he has? You guessed it! As the child spends time with his adopted family, he will learn what belongs to him. The same power, authority, and rights his parents have will eventually belong to the child, not because of what he does, but because he is in the family! The same is true for us in Christ. Jesus left us an inheritance, power and authority in His name, and nothing we do can steal what God has given to us. We need to discover what we have in Him.

Does **WWW.DO** increase your hope? You are permanently in the family of God. He hasn't left you hopeless. No. He has entrusted you with His Holy Spirit so that you can accomplish the work He has chosen specifically for you!

So, what are you going to do with this

> *When you know Who God is, Who you are, and What you have in Christ, you'll know what to* do.

profound wisdom? Will you encourage yourself so you can dream God-sized, God-inspired dreams?

David fought Goliath in 1 Samuel 17. Because his opponent was a giant, he could have felt defeated before he stepped up to the battle lines. David could have dwelled on all the things he was lacking, but he didn't! David was actually remembering all the ways God had helped him defeat enemies in the past. He knew whom he belonged to—*the army of the living God* (1 Samuel 17:26). He knew who he was in God's family. And he knew what belonged to Him—victory! Thus, David knew what to do!

David's response to the challenge before him is the perfect example of *WWW.DO* in action. He encouraged himself in the Lord by dwelling on the goodness of his God! It's so simple! The first step to taking back your hope is to remember the good things God has already done in your life!

Next, meditate on *who* God is. Who is He to you? He is not the originator of stealing, killing, or destroying in your life. John 10:10 declares that He is the one who brings life! You must have full confidence in your God to be successful at pursuing the dreams He has for you.

> **The way you view God will determine how you will stand in troubled times.**

Otherwise, your enemies may try to prevent you from achieving all that God has for you.

When our family is under a spiritual attack, we apply this verse to our daily life. *David was greatly distressed because the men were talking of stoning him; each one was bitter in spirit because of his sons and daughters. But David found strength in the Lord his God* (1 Samuel 30:6). We write down all the wonderful things God has done for our family: the salvations of family and friends, the miracles we have experienced, and other things that remind us of God's love for us. Then we post each wonder of God on our wall.

Now we can pray and thank God as we look at what He has done. Every time we feel discouraged, we can easily remember that God is for us and not against us. And every single time we are completely encouraged! It's absolutely true that *in the presence of the Lord is the fullness of joy* (Psalms 16:11 *paraphrased*).

Today, create a permanent record of God's goodness in your life. Write down your list, and hang it in a location where you can find it and read it daily; be strengthened by keeping your mind on the Lord. Every

> **When we remember what God has already done, suddenly, new struggles and battles don't seem as complicated or hard.**

moment holds the possibility for a miracle. Be watching for His hand at work, be faithful about writing those things down, and you will be prepared to encourage yourself whenever you are in a battle.

Daily, choose to dwell on your many blessings! Keep this in mind to fuel you.

> *WWW.DO—Who is God to you?* You belong to God! You are His child—adopted into the family of God! *Who* are you? *What* belongs to you? Remember your identity and your inheritance as a child of God. Take this knowledge to heart and *do* something with it! Return to this chapter as a reminder any time you feel discouraged during the *Stickie Dreamwall* process.

If you are encouraged and ready to uncover those old buried dreams, let's push up our sleeves; the fun part is coming!

But David encouraged himself in the Lord his God.

~ 1 SAMUEL 30:6 KJV

Part 3

BECOMING
A DREAMER

Chapter 11

TOTAL DREAM RECALL

*"The power of God will take you out of your own plans
and put you into the plan of God."*

~ SMITH WIGGLESWORTH

After you have done the hard work of taking your hope back by imprinting *WWW.DO* on your heart, uncovering your God-given dreams is the next step. It's often like searching for buried treasure. A lifetime of what-ifs, fears, and pessimism may have been piled on top of your dreams. Digging them out is a process.

My friend M.K. believed she had rediscovered her passion and dreams when she built her *Stickie Dreamwall.* But one night, as she was lying in her bed and looking at her dreams written out, God spoke to her, saying, "You are not dreaming big enough." *Wow*!

Her first pass identifying her dreams was a process of peeling back layers of many years of being influenced by worldly expectations, parents' dreams, and wounds from past failures. But after she rekindled her hope, God could then reveal the next level of dreams He had for her.

When my husband began to pursue his God-given dreams, he left his secure career and started his own consulting business. But that was only the first layer. During a two-month dry spell in his business, he had a chance to peel back another layer and rediscover his skills as an innovator. Instead of panicking about the future of his business and mentally running through all the worst-case scenarios, we asked God to help him use this time wisely.

As a result, my husband developed software to help his clients and he built iPhone apps for our ministry.

There is no better way to spend your life than on God's dreams for you.

Look at what God can do when we allow Him to peel back the layers of old beliefs and insecurities to reveal bigger and better dreams. I would have never dreamed that we would be where we are today. Are you ready to allow God to direct your steps?

My daughter is the voice of an animated character for our church. She loves it. At the last recording she did, we had the privilege of meeting the man, Sean McHargue, who designed the characters and helped develop the cartoon. He shared his journey with us, which is an inspirational dream revival story!

He always dreamed of a career in animation. As a kid, he drew comic strips and made up different characters. But when he saw the movie *Toy Story*, he believed, *There's no way I could ever be that good.* He believed the entire film was hand drawn—frame-by-frame. He felt there was no way he was talented enough to do that.

He quit. He gave up and attended school to become a nurse. I interjected, "A nurse? No way—you did *not*! How did your dreams change from drawing cartoons to becoming a nurse?" He knew that nursing would allow him to support a family, and he loved helping people. He had my attention, *Okay, I have to hear this story…Bring it.*

A few years later, while working in the nursing field, he discovered that *Toy Story* wasn't actually created the way he had originally assumed. It was created through animation software. This sparked the old, dead dream in him! He purchased inexpensive animation software and started experimenting with it. He peeled back layer after layer of uncovered hopes and dreams. In no time, he was out of nursing and into an animation career with our church!

Sean's life was eye-opening to my daughter. She stated, "Mom, I believe Dad is an artist in his heart and I am afraid he missed his calling. When we share Sean's journey with him, I bet Dad starts to use his art skill." Even she noticed that her dad had a third layer of God's dreams for him that he hadn't discovered yet.

What about you? Have you uncovered the first layer of what God has for you? This year, God awakened a dream in me that I had pushed to the back burner.

God gave my husband and I a vision for a ministry. But, immediately, I started reasoning through and analyzing this dream. My mind was racing with questions—*Will people use what God has placed on my heart to create? Will it be needed in our city? How will it be funded? Will the parking lot be big enough, or will it be such a small crowd we wouldn't need a parking lot?*

Months later, I was praying and worshipping God, and I heard God speak to me, "Do it because I AM worthy."

Although I still questioned how this dream would be possible, God peeled back layers of distraction to remind me He is Worthy for me to do it whether I understand it or not. He knew I would overanalyze it, so he made it very simple for me through a picture in my mind. He also gave me a purpose for the dream that even I can't overanalyze. Isn't it cool how God meets us where we are?

Wow. When you hear directly from God, it sets a fire on the inside to take the next step and then the next step until that dream is fulfilled! You don't have to seek counsel. You just know.

> **Jesus' death was far too much of a sacrifice to sit idly on the side.**

Dig deep for your dreams, because Christ is worthy and you are worth it. One of my sisters realized, "For the first time in a long time, I've learned how to dream again. It helped me realize how good God is. The truth that *everything* is possible with God finally sank in. It gave me vision and purpose and inspiration, and helped me realize that my life is worth more—that God has a purpose for me."

Jesus is the head, and we are the body. God uses us to fulfill His plan on this earth. We have to start dreaming again so that God can use us! Jesus's death was far too much of a sacrifice for us to sit idly on the side waiting and doing nothing in the meantime! He is worthy.

Pray today, and ask God to help you peel back every layer of doubt, fear, and lies that may be keeping you from dreaming God-sized dreams. Ask Him to show you His worth and why the mission He gave you is so important!

In his heart a man plans his course, but the LORD determines his steps.

~ PROVERBS 16:9

Chapter 12

DEFEAT DOUBT

"Doubt sees what currently is and no more.
Hope sees what can be but is not yet.
Faith sees what is and will be."

~ Rex Rouis

Your mind will fight against God's dreams for your life with reasoning, arguments, and analysis. Using natural "logic" will only get in the way of your effort to move forward on your God-given dreams.

Galatians 5:17 (NASB), *"For the flesh sets its desire against the Spirit, and the Spirit against the flesh; for these are in opposition to one another, so that you may not do the things that you please."* There is a constant battle between *me* (my mind and emotions) and the Holy Spirit. Our mind convinces us that we have to know the whole plan before we move forward. We need confirmation. We often need to experience results before we believe it.

But sometimes the facts can deceive us. When I was in the second grade, a boy sitting in the desk in front of me told the teacher that someone stole his quarter. The teacher looked around and stared hard at me. Now, we were dirt poor, and I probably looked the part, but I was honest; I did not take that quarter. Well, the teacher decided she wanted to take a look. She reasoned in her own mind that I was the problem. So she looked in my desk, and sure enough, there was that quarter. The evidence was there, and I was convicted beyond a reasonable doubt.

I knew I didn't take that quarter, but in the face of the "facts," even I started to wonder. The reality is, hard evidence is convincing. What you observe will move you. Your eyes and ears are faith funnels. What they take in is what your mind will believe. This is why reasoning and logic can get in the way of God's dreams for you. They can cause you to doubt your claim to victory in the Lord. God's plans do not operate on logic; He is much more powerful than that. Remember, when a piece of information does not line up with the God's truth, it is "trash."

When your doctor's report does not line up with the Bible—trash it. When your hopes are crushed because of your bank balance—trash it. God's word is the only truth that should matter to you. Scripture says that it is the *traditions of man that make the power of God of no effect*

(Mark 7:13 *paraphrased*). Traditionally, most people set their hopes and dreams on "facts" they experience with their five senses. It is the few who are walking a very narrow path and couldn't care less about a "fact" that sets itself up against the word of God who will prosper.

> **Your eyes and ears are faith funnels.**

When God called Moses to lead the people out of Egypt, he didn't show him the Promised Land or give him all the details of what it would take to get there. He asked Moses only to take a single step in faith and then wait on the next step. God didn't tell him all the obstacles that he would face. Would Moses have even led the people if he knew he personally would never arrive at the destination?

God doesn't tell us everything because following God requires *faith*. It's impossible to please Him without it (Hebrews 11:6a *paraphrased*). This builds on what we learned in the last section. When you place your hope in Him and remember all the amazing things He has already done in your life, you can overcome your doubts and pursue His dreams for you.

We recently built a *Stickie Dreamwall* with a local church. The church staff was already dreaming big—that was how they had the courage to start the church. But before long, doubts set in and their dreams became less clear. When we attempted the process with them, we began by remembering the big miracles that God had done in their lives. One of the families reminded everyone of a huge miracle that God had done; He had saved their almost-dead son! Today, he is alive and well. Everyone on the team had forgotten about that miracle. Once they started remembering God's wonderful works, He exploded their dreaming! Their doubts began to dissolve, and they truly knew that *all* things are possible with God! They built their *Dreamwall*. Keeping the wonders of God in the front of your mind on a daily basis brings focus.

Your doubts and rationale will lead you astray. Following God is not something you can justify; you do it by faith alone! *The mind of sinful man is death, but the mind controlled by the Spirit is life and peace* (Romans 8:6).

Trust that God directs your steps. This implies that you are off the couch. Scripture doesn't say that God will pick you up and place you on the perfect path where your hands never get dirty. God asks you to consider your relationship with Him superior to your fears. All you need is the faith to take a few steps.

> George Muller is one of my favorite historical figures not because he was a pastor or a preacher, but because he believed God's word to be true. He ran an orphanage in Bristol, England. How he got there is a great journey you should read. One day, he found himself without

food for three hundred hungry kids. He prayed. He trusted in God and encouraged every one of those kids to do the same. That same morning, a milk truck broke down in front of the orphanage. The truck driver knew the milk would spoil and offered it to the orphanage so he could get it off of his truck. Additionally, the local baker felt compelled that very morning to bring a load of baked goods to George's orphanage. The stories of faith and his reliance on the word of God above his circumstances go on and on. God never failed. [1]

And without faith it is impossible to please God.

~ HEBREWS 11:6A

---

1 Janet and Geoff Benge, *George Muller: The Guardian of Bristol's Orphans* (Seattle: YWAM Publishing, 1999).

Chapter 13

DON'T DROWN IN COMFORT

"Observe carefully the manner in which the world is going and go the opposite."

~ LAWRENCE RAY (SHERI'S GREAT-GRANDDAD)

Do you long to discover God's miraculous power through your life? Jesus's disciple Peter certainly experienced His crazy magnificent power!

You can read about his amazing experience in Matthew 14. The disciples were on the boat when a storm came. The boat was taking a beating. The disciples were afraid.

> **Search for the rough waters, because that is where you will get to walk on water in the power of God!**

Let's stop for a second and imagine being on this boat. The boat probably had the capacity of ten people—so it's a small boat. Waves were crashing on the sides, and water was pouring into the boat. Maybe the boat was at risk of breaking apart. Maybe it was all the disciples could do to hold on and not fall overboard. Otherwise, why were they in so much fear?

Back to the story…

So Jesus came walking out on the water. Peter was the only one on the boat who asked Jesus if he could walk on the water. The other disciples probably presumed Peter was crazy! Their minds might have worried about what would happen to Peter when he stepped out of the boat. *Will he sink? Will the waves take him under? Will we ever gaze at Peter again?*

Peter wasn't considering any of those things. He was ready to walk on water! *"Come," Jesus declared. Then Peter got down out of the boat, walked on the water, and came toward Jesus* (Matthew 14:29).

All the other disciples were fearfully clinging to a sinking ship. But being in the ship was probably their comfort zone. Although their ship was basically drowning, they decided to embrace what they knew. They held onto the familiar when it clearly led to destruction. Their tightly clutched grip on the

> **Ruts can prevent you from experiencing miracles.**

sinking boat caused them to miss out on the impressive miracle Peter experienced. Their rut kept them from experiencing a life-altering miracle! Peter walked on water!

Why would you stay in your bubble—perhaps a sinking ship—and miss the opportunity to experience mighty miracles? My husband always tells me, "Sheri, search for the rough waters, because that is where you will get to walk on water in the power of God!"

What is your comfort zone?

> For my husband, it was the wonderful career he left when he started his own business. He was successful at his company, and his job allowed him to provide for us easily. A few years back, however, God had given my husband a vision that he was trying to grow, but he had this concrete ceiling above his head. God revealed to him that the ceiling was his reliance on himself and his career. While my husband felt as though his career was his foundation, God showed him that his career was a ceiling, and God was the floor from which he could grow to his full potential.

With that in mind, once we knew God had released my husband from his old career and we were in unity on the matter, he left his secure job for an adventure I could have never predicted. He leaped out of the rut and into the land of the unknown, but he was dreaming again! His comfort zone was shattered.

Maybe your familiar territory is sticking with your job of ten-plus years because it is known, safe, and secure. You earn enough money to enjoy life—most of the time. But your heart's desire is to start your own business. However, you are afraid of failing, of not being able to provide for your family, or how people will label you. This fear can keep you in a rut.

Jesus tells us again and again not to be afraid. In Matthew 14:27, when they were in the middle of a storm, He exhorted His disciples, *"Take courage! It is I. Don't be afraid."* It's time to dig deep and define what limits are holding you back from God's dreams. You can't move out of your comfort zone if you haven't identified it.

Maybe your security revolves around the fact that you are a working

> **Fear and small thinking will keep you from experiencing the amazing miracles of God!**

mom who has been called to homeschool your children. However, your family needs your income or your children enjoy school friends and activities. Maybe you doubt that you are equipped or smart enough to teach your own children. Trusting in what you know can cause you to miss God's desires for your life.

Now, don't misunderstand what I am saying. God can still work in your life. He will meet you where you are. But wouldn't you rather step out in faith and do what He wants you to do? Stop focusing on what could fail and imagine what could succeed! Focus on Philippians 4:13, *I can do everything through him who gives me strength. Nothing* can stand in your way because God is for you!

Get outside your comfort zone because God is worthy of you taking a risk!

By now, I hope you're deciding, *"I will not settle for complacency anymore. Limiting God in my life is no long acceptable!"* But you're also likely to wonder how in the world to change.

Once you have identified your comfort zone, firmly commit to having a zero tolerance for living in it. Did you commit? Okay—now, determine the very first step to climb out of your rut.

> **Stop focusing on what could go wrong and imagine what could go right!**

If praying aloud for someone makes you run far away and avoid these situations at all costs, start refusing to run away when future opportunities arise. Take it a step further, you can now step out in faith and initiate praying aloud for someone. Ask if you can pray for him or her. Start with your parents, a friend, your spouse, a child, your kids, or the cashier at a store. Then don't stop. People you ask may not react the way you expect them to. Do not let that deter you from stepping outside of your comfort zone. Keep taking steps out of it.

Stepping into unfamiliar territory requires hard work. If it were easy, there would be no such thing as a comfort zone! It takes a conscious daily effort not to return to it. Doing hard things is, well... *hard*. There is no way around it. Unknown circumstances and new ventures can be scary.

> **Trusting in what you know can cause you to miss God's desires for your life.**

It's easy to continue to lie on the couch each evening and become lazy and fat, but it's hard work to look for an active hobby or exercise partner to help you keep physically fit. It's easy to hide and head straight into your house every time you return home from work; it's hard to reach out to your neighbors and develop a community. It's easy to order the same rotation of takeout meals each week; it's hard work to plan, prepare, cook, serve, and clean up a homemade dinner. But it's so worth it.

And *God* is worth it! He is worthy of *all* you have. He is worthy of the hard labor. Remembering this will keep you motivated.

Your view of God will be strengthened as you step outside your comfort zone to live by truth and faith!

> ### *Truly I tell you, if you have faith as small as a mustard seed, you can say to this mountain, Move from here to there, and it will move. Nothing will be impossible for you.*
>
> ~ MATTHEW 17:20

Part 4

CREATING YOUR DREAMWALL

Chapter 14

STICKIE DREAMWALL

"Never let the fear of striking out keep you from playing the game."

~ Babe Ruth

I pray that by now God has given you inspiring revelations about the type of dreamer you are today. Wherever you are on your journey, I know that you aspire to be a dream lifter. But inspiration and revelation will only get you so far. Now it is time to move that motivation momentum into practical action.

While reading the previous sections of this book, you may have been wondering what exactly is a *Stickie Dreamwall*. It has obviously impacted the lives of many people, but how? Well, you're about to find out.

Stickie Dreamwall is more than a process of uncovering the buried dreams of your heart and learning to hope and trust in God. It's also a tangible representation of what God has done in your life and where He is taking you. It is a tool to help you keep the momentum going and a way to share your dreams with others.

The detailed steps outlined in this section have not only inspired countless people to dream again, but the process itself has further ignited their hope and spurred them on in their pursuit of those dreams. Thousands of dreams have been realized and generations have been changed forever as a result.

The *Stickie Dreamwall* process is so simple and so natural that your dreams will spill out of you and start taking shape in no time. You are literally going to create a wall where your dreams are on display clearly before you. With this prominent visual tool in front of you each day, you will have a tangible way to track the progress of your dreams and a constant source of encouragement to take the next step. This process will clarify your next steps.

> Lisa and her family completed *Stuck* and built their *Dreamwall* process over one year ago. This process has significantly impacted our friend Lisa's daughter. One of her daughters included a dream of writing a children's discipleship curriculum. Because she courageously posted her dreams on the family *Dreamwall* and faithfully completed each next

step, she was perfectly prepared when Lisa's family pastor asked her to write a series for the children of their church! Lisa and her family are praising God for what He has done in their daughter's life!

You may be hesitating, *Why should I build a Stickie Dreamwall, Sheri? That's just silly. I don't enjoy the idea of my dreams posted on my wall. It's embarrassing, too messy, and childish.*

I can assure you that your dreams will be more likely realized when you have a physical record of your next steps. It is a daily reminder staring you in the face.

> **Reinvigorate your life for purpose!**

I believe that through this process you will discover God's direction in your life more clearly. Most people are overwhelmed with obligations, distractions, and even "good" goals that keep their focus away from God's *best* plan for them. The Bible says that God chose you before the world began for a specific purpose. Don't spend one more day postponing the important dreams He has for you. In Jeremiah 1, God filled Jeremiah's mouth with words to influence kingdoms and nations and He is doing that for you too. Reinvigorate your life for purpose! Engage your imagination. Live on the edge. Ignite God's dreams. Change the world!

> **"You gain strength, courage, and confidence by every experience in which you really stop to look fear in the face. You must do the thing you think you cannot do."**
>
> ~ ELEANOR ROOSEVELT

If you ask my sister Kathleen how *Stickie Dreamwall* process has affected her, she always responds, "Making a *Dreamwall* changed my life. I learned to dream again, and I don't plan to stop—ever!"

The movie *Field of Dreams* has a famous quote, "If you build it, they will come." Today, decide and commit to build it. Do it for yourself, but also do it for those who are following you. When you build it, others will join you.

Stickie Dreamwall Shopping List

1. Corkboard
2. Push Pins
3. Double-sided tape
4. Blue sticky notes
5. Yellow sticky notes
6. A different colored marker or pen for each family member
7. Folder or binder to keep completed steps

Molly K. Allis Story

"About a year ago, I lost sight of who I was and where I was going. It did not take me long to figure out that having no vision was not an option in my life. However, I was about to graduate from grad school, and my whole life up to that point had been mapped out by what I was supposed to do. I always wanted to do what I was 'supposed to,' but never before had I gotten to the point where it was open ended.

At that time, my life was also getting turned upside down by rediscovering my identity in Jesus. To be honest, I had no idea how my identity and dreams collided. Prior to this experience, my dreams were based off of what I was good at or what I ought to be doing. But I had never sat down and asked myself what I *wanted* to do or what I imagined myself working toward until the day I die. That is when Sheri told me about the *Stickie Dreamwall* process.

Honestly, it took me about two weeks before I finally sat down and did it. I was ashamed that this 'over-ambitious, talented girl' had no idea where I wanted to be going anymore. While at the store purchasing supplies for my *Dreamwall*, I stalled by looking for just the right color sticky notes to post on my wall. I stood in the aisle determining, *Hmm wait, which shade of blue do I like?*

Once home with the supplies, I sat on my bed for fifteen minutes pondering. Finally, I grabbed a marker, and my dreams *exploded*! Who knew there were so many in there? Why had I waited so long—this was easy! Dreams—check! Next steps—check! Stick it to the wall—check!

Something started to stir in me; my heart was overflowing. I was not done, but the wall was filled. I started on a new space on the wall...*dream bigger*! Good thing I bought the value pack of sticky notes!

This process made me realize that there is so much already in me. When I put it on the wall for me and everyone else to notice, my dreams started to become reality. Yeah, you read that right! I have not achieved one of my big dreams, yet, but give me a few more months. I have already completed many of the steps on my wall.

I am capable of dreaming God-sized dreams, working hard, and living out the reality of His dreams for me. Someone once shared, *'Commitment is the ability to carry out the resolution after the hype is gone.'* The *Stickie Dreamwall* is my commitment to the Lord that I will choose every day to walk in His calling for my life. My calling is huge because my God is huge!"

—

Before I formed you in the womb I knew you, before you were born I set you apart.

~ JEREMIAH 1:5

Chapter 15

DREAMSTORM

"Don't limit yourself. You can go as far as your mind lets you. Remember, what you believe is what you will achieve."

~ MARY KAY ASH

Roll up your sleeves; it's time to build your personal *Stickie Dreamwall*! Are you excited? I am! Now, don't be intimidated. It might be hard to let loose and dream. Remember, God will guide you. Don't worry about anyone's opinions of your dreams—including you! This is a simple way to trust God. Now, let's *Dreamstorm*!

Stickie Dreamwall **Ground Rules**
For a fruitful outcome, before you launch your *Dreamstorming* session establish basic ground rules. Many have had our dreams suppressed by opinions of others,

or been wounded by teasing and insecurity. Therefore, create an accepting and encouraging environment to foster trust and belief in those participating.

Rule #1—Anything Goes

Any dream is valid. This is where you will discover that one person's dreams will ignite another's that might have been on hold. Resist the urge to say or *think* these phrases: That's impossible, that's not practical, or that's already been done. These types of comments should be strictly prohibited. Truly—anything goes. This means that you have to withhold your opinion. You can't bring reasoning, practicality, and analytics into the Dreamstorming session. Reasoning will come in later in the process, but for now, it stifles the process. The Bible says that all things are possible, so who are we to judge any idea, regardless how far out or unattainable it may seem?

Your group will not share their dreams if they expect their ideas will be rejected or scrutinized. If you want your loved ones to share the desires of their heart, then zip your lips and allow them to express themselves freely. Create an atmosphere of acceptance.

Rule #2—No Complimenting

Certain ideas will immediately impress the group. Others will not. Avoid discouraging any dreams with cautionary comments. Also do not praise one idea more enthusiastically than another.

Accept each idea in the same manner to avoid giving the impression that some have better dreams than others. This is harder than it sounds, because a few goals are guaranteed to spark more excitement than others. However, be gentle so that each person feels that his or her dreams are equally important and worthwhile. Otherwise, your participants will shut down and close their heart from the group and you can forget hearing their dreams again!

Rule #3—Inspire and Encourage

As dreams emerge, inspire deeper digging with questions that start with *when*, *where*, and *who*. You could ask, "When did you first have this dream?" or "Where were you when you discovered this dream?"

This is not the time to ask "how" or "why." When people look forward at a big goal, it can be intimidating to consider the amount of work it will take to accomplish the dream. But, when we break it down into baby steps—I will explain this later in the *Stickie Dreamwall* process—the impossible suddenly becomes achievable.

"As a twenty-something, dreaming is hard! I am finally able to dream again, but after more than ten years of suppressing my dreams, it's hard to keep moving forward. You don't desire this to happen in your family. You hope they will be able to talk about their dreams. You desire that they will pursue the dreams of their heart, right? Then help your family dream bigger, help them take steps to fulfill the dreams they have today so they will have the confidence to pursue their dreams tomorrow." ~ Elizabeth

Rule #4—Watch Body Language
Nonverbal communication can be as damaging as spoken criticism. Any gestures or facial expressions that have the potential to inhibit someone from dreaming are not allowed.

Rule #5—Celebrate
Dreamstorming is an opportunity to celebrate the dreams of your heart God revealed. Don't let the atmosphere become strained or uncomfortable. Praise God!

Now that we all understand the rules that will promote relationships and imagination in your *Dreamstorming* session, these are the three steps to a productive discussion to uncover all the buried dreams in your group.

Step 1—Remember God

Before we begin dreaming, we need to remember together the wonderful things God has done in our lives. Chapter 10 talks in depth about this subject. Start here. It gets everyone talking and really sharing. Grab a stack of yellow sticky notes and a wall or white board where they will stick (use tape if you have to). Ask one or more of these questions to your family, small group, or even yourself:

- What are some of the amazing things God has done in my life?
- In what ways has God blessed me that have changed my life forever?
- What acts of God in His word inspire me the most?
- How has God used other people in my life to move and motivate me?
- How has God surprised me by His presence in my life?

Write down everything you or others in the group say as fast as you can with a permanent marker on the yellow sticky notes. Abbreviate, write quickly, and press everything onto your wall or your white board until the discussion starts to slow down. Conversations may flow down many rabbit trails. Let it. Allow God to move and to stir you through the laughter, tears, and excitement. He is truly a great God, and we never take enough time to remember how faithful He has been in our lives.

Before step 2, ask God to direct your mind, actions, and steps. Ask Him to reveal the dreams He has placed in your heart.

Step 2—Dreamstorm

Next, grab sticky notes. We use blue ones. You'll also need markers. Consider using a different colored marker for each person.

Pass out a sticky pad to each person in your family, or have one or two people writing on behalf of everyone.

122

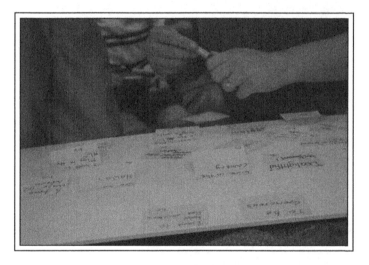

I highly recommend that everyone over the age of twelve have his or her own pad to write on.

We have found that adults and young adults are more inhibited with their ideas. However, younger children are amazing dreamers! They almost always

inspire dreams in others. Encourage everyone to participate.

Then let the dreams fly, and write down **ALL** ideas as they come. No idea is too small or too crazy. Consider the deepest desires of your

> **Open your heart to allow God to reignite the dreams He has given you.**

heart. Include the ways you are excited to contribute. Dreamstorm and capture any and every dream now or in the past. If you need help getting started, ask yourself or your group these questions:

- What would you like to change in the world?
- If you could change something for the better, what would it be?
- What is going on in the world today that you absolutely love?
- What is going on in this world that you cannot stand?
- What have you always desired to do?
- What is something you do that makes you literally lose track of time?
- What do you believe you can improve in the world?

Open your heart to allow God to reignite His dreams within you. Dig deep. For those uncomfortable with dreaming, chances are their first response is not going to be their true heart's desire. Remember the unreasonable childhood dreams you dismissed. Uncover your buried dreams. Dig out the dreams others advised were impossible. Remember the rules we discussed in this chapter. Don't be a dream killer or a dream keeper in the first phase of the *Stickie Dreamwall* process. Allow yourself to realize that we cannot envision what God can do with an impractical dream.

It may end up that you no longer hope to fulfill any of your childhood dreams. But the process of remembering and saying your childhood dreams can stir up a passion for the dreams you have now. Do not be distracted by how you will accomplish a certain dream or how dumb your dream must sound to everyone else. Continue dreaming until you literally cannot conceive another. This may take a while. Take your time and exhaust every dream. Leave it and come back as necessary.

> **Dig out the dreams others advised were impossible.**

Write down each and every unfulfilled dream one at a time on a separate blue sticky note—and press them on an open area on a wall or whatever vertical surface you have. You can also lay a poster board or corkboard on a table and hang it on the wall when you are finished. Use tape or push pins as necessary to ensure your sticky notes stay on the surface.

Don't be afraid to think outside the box. Pick a place that is unique to your family. Ensure it is viewable to each family member. Go for it.

Step 3—Share It

Dreamstorming is a family or community affair. These steps are great fun with friends or family. Pull them together. Tell them you need their help to uncover the dreams of your heart. Who can resist that request? Gather whoever is at your house; invite your spouse, your family, your extended family, or your neighbors; sit down and simply start sharing your dreams.

Don't be embarrassed for others to know your deepest dreams. Yes, posting my deepest desires on our *Stickie Dreamwall* for the whole world to observe was a bit embarrassing at first, but was also freeing. Now, I'm experiencing God take me step-by-step, every day, in that direction. When I was willing to lay my own life down and admit His dreams for me, I began to really notice His power freely at work in my life.

Jemma Stemmons' Story

"My husband, Scott, and I often lie in bed and dream about many things. But one night, through some great friends of ours, we learned how to prioritize and bring to life our dreams!

Our friends Tracy, Sheri, and their girls joined us for pizza. During our conversation, Tracy simply asked what dreams God had planted in my heart. At first, I couldn't say anything. Of course we had dreams, but we had never shared them openly with anyone. Scott threw out a couple of things, and Sheri asked if we had sticky notes. Scott shared more, and then I began to share. Sheri continued to write and then post the sticky notes on our wall. Our *Dreamwall* was born!

We talked more, and the Yates encouraged us to pray and ask God to give our dreams next steps. Scott and I climbed into bed with such excitement! Again, we had talked before about all of the things that were posted that night, but I can't express the impact it made being able to view them. God has continued to give us dreams. They are no longer things we just talk about. We post them and pray, and God gives us our next steps. We've also been able to celebrate many of these dreams coming true!

Our girls were only five and two at the time, but we invited them on this dream journey with us. Our five-year-old had watched me get up and run several days a week. Scott brought our girls to watch me run a 5K one Saturday, and Abigail mentioned that she wanted to start running with me.

Later that week, I came in from a run, and she asked me for a sticky note. She walked over to our *Dreamwall* and began to write something. She got a piece of tape and posted her newest dream. Abigail wanted to run a race with Mommy. We talked about what she needed to do in order to run a race. She got excited, so we posted her next steps and off we went.

Sure, some of the dreams of a child seem impossible—and even ridiculous—to you and me, but what might God do with our children when we tell them, "If God wants you to do this, it is possible"? We took a risk on looking weird to others and the risk of Abigail failing, but we helped her pursue some of her dreams.

Abigail's dream came true. She and I did the Princess Run and the Red Bud Classic, and now she is asking when we can do another one. She's also seen several other dreams become a reality. She plays golf with Daddy, returned to Disney World, and has been on TV! We will continue to encourage her to post and pursue her God-given dreams. I know she will accomplish many more dreams come true this year!

Because she is pursuing her God-given dreams, Abigail knows the power of her God! Not only does she encourage Scott's faith and mine, her faith has inspired countless others. Abigail led a little girl to Christ this year. She so naturally shared her heart and love for Jesus and changed a little girl's life forever. She prays big prayers. Scott got to baptize Abigail in June. Getting baptized was another one of her dreams. What a special day for us all! We pray that she continues to know God more and more this year. May she continue to walk in His truth, and may His love continue to flow from her life to impact others for His glory."

For I know the plans I have for you, declares the Lord, plans to prosper you and not to harm you, plans to give you hope and a future.

~ JEREMIAH 29:11

Chapter 16

BUILDING MOMENTUM

"As you seek God, your best strategy is to set short-term goals so that He can give you long-term victories."

~ CRAIG GROESCHEL, CHAZOWN

We fail to accomplish our dreams when a lack of momentum discourages us. We are going to overcome this barrier together. The first step in keeping momentum is to gain momentum. You are going to build energy by first sorting your dreams into similar categories, either as a group or as individuals, and then prioritizing them by ease of attainment. This is how we build momentum!

Sort—Identify Similar Purposes and Objectives

After you have finished Dreamstorming, sort and group your sticky notes by similarity. Create a column on your *Stickie Dreamwall* for each category of like-kind dreams. For example, when my family sorted our sticky notes into categories, we realized we only had five categories between the seven of us! Many times, your dreams will fall into similar categories such as physical fitness, business goals, spiritual growth, academic achievements, community involvement, etc.

Is there a pattern in your passions? Do you notice a block of sticky notes all related to a similar purpose or objective?

Our iKAN Ministry team and I completed a *Stickie Dreamwall* with a small group recently. Most of these people had never met. We discovered that, unknown to anyone in the room, almost 65 percent of the group had a dream to lead or be involved with corporate worship. Everyone was blown away. We were not only mutually encouraged but, with unity, we found momentum.

Grouping will help people form teams and compel progress together. For instance, a family member dreamed to create modest but attractive swimwear. Another person had an interest in fashion design. The two of them chose to work together on accomplishing their dreams. Because of their combined effort, I am confident that someday you will be able to purchase their designs!

Prioritize—Identify Low-Hanging Fruit

Low-hanging fruit is easy to pick. In order to foster momentum, we need to find dreams that are easy to reach.

After you have sorted all of your dreams into similar categories, each person in the group should identify no more than *three* dreams from the *Stickie Dreamwall* (regardless of the category or type of dream) that are the easiest to accomplish. You can identify dreams that are easy to reach by finding those that are simple. Perhaps it's the dream that requires only one or two action steps to bring it to reality. Dreams that are easy to realize can be accomplished quickly. In other words, you may only need to walk across the room to accomplish it.

> Our friend Joe is excited about developing an ATV ministry where leaders can come together in a remote and neutralizing environment to be refreshed, refocused, and built up in truth. He also wants to ensure his daughters are grounded in God's truth, and he wants to retire and start a second career. Which of these dreams are low-hanging fruit for Joe? You got it. Of course, the simplest and easiest dream for Joe to accomplish is to disciple his own daughters. He can start tomorrow with little to no

investment. Who knows where pursuing this vision will lead him? At a minimum, it will create undeniable momentum that will catapult this dream into a reality.

These simple and easy dreams you identified are your top priority. Clarify that these dreams are your focus. Move them to the top of the group of similar dreams. Star them; wrap them in crochet; or spray paint them gold. Whatever you need to do to recognize these top three dreams as important—do that.

Place the sticky notes with those dreams that are more difficult to accomplish (e.g., a ten-year-old wants to "start an orphanage") at the bottom of the *Dreamwall* within the category.

> **Less is more.**

As the dreams classified as "low-hanging fruit" are accomplished, they will generate the momentum you need to dig into the next layer of dreams. I encourage you to move the dreams you have accomplished to a *remembrance board*. Keep them within eyeshot. Being able to constantly remind yourself that you have now made it off the couch will help motivate you to make it around the block again and again.

As you accomplish the simpler goals, move to the next level of dreams that are perhaps a little more complex and require a little more time up the wall and into the top priority group. Never get more than three priorities moving at a time. After all, you still have a life to manage. Maybe you are in school, working, or managing a household, etc. If you get too many things started at one time, it will only create a burden.

Less is more. The more we narrow our focus, the more able we are to create movement. Each individual focuses on only three dreams at a time until they are realized. This narrowing and focusing creates energy and momentum.

Now that you are focused on a manageable number of dreams, consider adding elements to your *Stickie Dreamwall* to enhance these first goals. For example, you might choose a relevant verse from Scripture to accompany each dream. Or, for the more visually motivated, add a photo that represents the dream next to the sticky note. Get creative.

Now that you *are* organized, let's begin identifying next steps…

The Lord will guide you always.

~ ISAIAH 58:11

Chapter 17

STICKY STEPS

*"Faith is taking the first step even when you
don't see the whole staircase."*

~ MARTIN LUTHER KING, JR.

We should have identified three key dreams for each person that can be easily accomplished. It's time for the next step on your *Stickie Dreamwall* to turn your dreams into actions. It is simpler than you envision. Grab sticky notes in a different color from the previous session.

Define the Next Steps
My husband always says, *"Man has his plans, but God directs his steps; and by that, God plans for you to be off the couch."* To inspire yourself in the game, keep the process

simple. What I am about to show you is as straightforward as it gets.

For each of the dreams you have categorized as "fairly easy to accomplish," ask yourself this question: *What is the next thing I need to do to accomplish this dream?*

Determine the simplest next action step. For example, if your dream is to share Christ with the world, your very next step might be to introduce yourself to your neighbors. If one of your dreams is to start a running club on a college campus, your next step might be to research existing running clubs online. If you have a vision to start a business, your next step might be to write down *what drove you to* take this leap of faith.

You may be tempted to write several next steps, but resist the urge! You may tempted to write down next steps on goals other than your top three, but don't do it! It's when we look at all the steps in accumulation that dreams become overwhelming.

> **Your spiritual enemy wants to distract and discourage you from God's dreams. Keep the enemy behind you with simple successes.**

On the other hand, when we take the smallest next step possible on the simplest dreams to accomplish, we obtain real and steady progress toward achieving our dreams. The smaller the step, the less likely you are to get distracted. Baby steps are not overwhelming. Three of our family members recently ran our first half-marathon. Our first step was to purchase an app for our phones to get us off the couch. This program didn't ask us to run around the block on the first day. We started with a short walk. Before you knew it, we were all running three miles, then six, then ten. It wasn't easy, but each next step led us to our dream. We are scheduled to run our second half-marathon soon, and it all started with a few simple first steps!

Take the Next Steps
Before you do anything else—take the steps you have outlined above! Don't start on any other dreams. Focus on the next thing on the three easiest to accomplish dreams. Get to work on these next steps.

"I dream of men who take the next step instead of worrying about the next thousand steps."

~ THEODORE ROOSEVELT

Take close aim before you pull the trigger. Now fire! Take off and complete the next step for each of the "low-hanging fruit" dreams or pick only one to focus on. Unless you skip or replace this next step, progress no further until you have accomplished it. Sometimes, you might miss the mark and write down the wrong step or take a step that is too big. No problem. Stop and narrow in on the right step.

Keep the steps as small as possible. Small steps are easier to get done. Compare it to physical fitness. The first few days or weeks of physical training are not fun. As momentum builds, you will desire to press forward more and more. Energy grows with momentum. Execute the next thing in front of you, and that's it. Now is not the time to consider the other steps to be completed.

> **Using the *Stickie Dreamwall* process to take one step at a time makes what appears impossible achievable! When the world says it is impossible, taking baby steps toward your dreams will shatter your disbelief.**

—

Remember that no plan is free from enemy fire. If something blocks you from completing this first next step, then do something different. Do not lose momentum. Find another way. Maneuver over, under, or around obstacles. It might be hard, because this may be the first time you truly have had to trust God with something you can't do on your own. God is worthy of the pursuit of your dreams, and He will direct your steps. You have to get off the couch.

Why should you stay so focused on the next thing? Your spiritual enemy wants to distract and discourage you from God's dreams. Keep the enemy behind you with simple successes.

If you remain faithful in the smallest action, God will produce an immense work in your heart. Diligent faithfulness in these small, next-step actions will build your hope and faith for the subsequent steps. Movement creates momentum!

Remember Newton's first law, the law of inertia: An object at rest will remain at rest unless acted on by an unbalanced force. An object in motion continues in motion with the same speed and in the same direction unless acted upon by an unbalanced force.

> **Movement creates momentum!**

After you have finished the next step, take the second, third, and fourth steps, and so on…one at a time. Before you know it, you have accomplished a dream!

"Don't judge each day by the harvest you reap, but by the seeds you plant."
~ ROBERT LOUIS STEVENSON

Contemplating the big picture of the unbelievable multitude of steps will only overburden you and possibly limit you from achieving your dreams. Don't do that. Remember to focus only on the very next thing.

—

Stephanie Davis-Reed's Story

Our friend Stephanie Davis-Reed is a dream lifter. Stephanie is a pastor and owns a business, appropriately named "Dream Lifters." She is no stranger to the hard work required to achieve dreams.

Stephanie is possibly the most physically fit woman I have ever met. More important, she is spiritually fit. How does she accomplish so much? She would answer, "Diligence every day." She watches what she eats *every day*. She is physically active *every day*. She pursues her dreams *every day*. She encourages others *every day*. She pursues God *every day*.

Stephanie has also dreamed of becoming a speaker for Women of Faith. She didn't start by filling out an application. She started by serving. For the last thirteen years, without any expectation and without fail, Stephanie has been promoting and volunteering for Women of Faith behind the scenes. Every year, she invites a hoard of women to share with them the conference that has made such an impact in her life: Women of Faith. Every year, she sits a little closer to the stage. This year, she told her mom, "We are on the front row, and there is only one more step God is preparing me for."

Little did she know that within a few hours, she would be up on that stage doing push-ups! Christine Caine was speaking, and she asked for assistance from the audience. She invited Stephanie up onto the stage. In typical form, Christine commented, "Wow, great arms! Do you do push-ups?"

The next thing you know, a push-up contest was "on" between Christine and Stephanie in front of twenty thousand women! Even more impressive are the three women in Stephanie's group who gave their lives to Christ that day. Praise God for how He is showing Stephanie she is on the right track and guiding her in small daily steps toward

His dreams for her. Praise God that Stephanie consistently pursues her relationship with Him and shows her love for others—every day.

—

Whoever can be trusted with very little can also be trusted with much.

~ LUKE 16:10

Chapter 18

STICK WITH IT

*"The future belongs to those who believe
in the beauty of their dreams."*

~ ELEANOR ROOSEVELT

When you give your dreams the attention and prominence in your living space that they deserve, you'll be surprised at how easily steady progress comes. You'll need to keep the momentum moving so that you can finish strong and reach all of God's plans for you. Start today. Here's how:

Start today.

Celebrate

Each time you complete another step, celebrate your progress with your family and friends. Then remove that step's sticky note and file it in a notebook. This will be a source of great encouragement to look back on and remember your accomplishments.

You will continue to meet with your family or friends and share progress and repeat next steps until this dream is realized. As small dreams are realized, move on to the more difficult ones and follow the same process.

Share your accomplishments. This will motivate and encourage others. Reward accomplishments. Ask for guidance when stuck. Find counsel from experts in the area of your hopes and dreams. For example, in our efforts to help our kids write and publish their first song, we sought out a singer/songwriter who would mentor them throughout

150

the process. The oldest child was only ten years old when they started pursuing this dream, and it has now been achieved. This motivated Kathleen (from chapter 3) to write a song. Sharing our successes motivates others.

As your dreams are accomplished, move onto bigger and better ones!

> How do you know if you are pursing the right aspirations?

First, do not worry. Trust God. If you are in relationship with the Lord and renewing your mind, you can trust that He's planting desires in your heart.

151

Second, ask God to turn your selfish desires toward His visions for you. Proverbs 16:9 says, *"In his heart a man plans his course, but the Lord determines his steps."* Ask God to direct your steps toward the desires that He wants you to pursue and to curb the desires for the dreams your flesh longs to accomplish.

Third, remember simply to acknowledge Jesus in everything you do. If you are acknowledging Jesus in everything, you can be certain He will direct your steps. His Word says, *"Trust in the Lord with all your heart and lean not on your own understanding; in all your ways acknowledge him, and he will make your paths straight"* (Proverbs 3:5–6).

Lastly, Colossians 3:15 reads, *"Let the peace of Christ rule in your hearts."* If you don't have a deep internal peace about something, don't do it!

Press forward. Physically hang your *Stickie Dreamwall*— so it's easy to access. Maybe you are saying, "Oh we won't forget. I don't need to hang it. It's too embarrassing." But oh, you will forget! Keep it before your eyes. Hanging it for the whole family to view will increase momentum and energy.

Another way to create progress is to meet as a family every day, every few days, or at least once a week. Share what you have accomplished, and take time to celebrate together. Take finished steps off the wall and keep them in a folder or binder as a reminder of how far you have come. Find the next small step together and encourage each other to complete it. Once you accomplish the dream, take the blue sticky note down and list it on the things God has done in your life. (We discussed remembering what God has done in your life in chapter 12.)

Don't let this call to imagine and dream again die and be placed back on the shelf. Dreams are not meant to collect dust.

> If you don't have a deep internal peace about something, just don't do it!

Do something with it. Set a time line. Be specific. Start today. Purchase sticky notes. In the next twenty-four hours, start writing down your hopes and visions, have a discussion over dinner tonight...do *something*.

Don't be afraid to invite others into your journey. Those who love you most can support you, pray for you, encourage you, and help you do more than you could ever do on your own! Write down a list of people you trust to share your *Dreamwall* with this week. Many are suffering from dream suppression. Revive someone's hope for a future today!

My dreams were so deeply buried that sharing them was the most painful, yet freeing, thing I've done! Allowing others to know the deepest desires of my heart made me vulnerable, but once I was out of my comfort zone, nothing could stop me!

"It takes a lot of courage to show your dreams to someone else."
~ ERMA BOMBECK

The future of our world is really in the hands of a few. Everyone is called, but only few will do what it takes to relentlessly pursue the hopes and vision God has placed in their heart!

I refuse to be buried with God's calling for my life unfinished! Join me in this pursuit to start and finish strong.

Enter through the narrow gate. For wide is the gate and broad is the road that leads to destruction, and many enter through it. But small is the gate and narrow the road that leads to life, and only a few find it.
~ MATTHEW 7:13-14

LIVING THE DREAM

"Visionary people face the same problem everyone else faces; but rather than get paralyzed by their problems, visionaries immediately commit themselves to finding a solution."

~ BILL HYBELS

Bill Hybels is arguably one of the best leaders of all time. He has changed the way the Church does church. He had a dream, and when you look into his eyes and hear him talk, you know that it is still alive. Bill believes the local Church is the hope of the world. We agree.

We also know that you are the hope of the local Church! There is one question Bill asks that we continue to ask. *"Where is the nose of your plane?"* In order to keep your dream alive, you need to ask the same question continually: *Are you gaining or losing altitude in your life?*— Is your marriage gaining or losing altitude? Are your kids gaining or losing altitude? Is the nose of the plane of your relationship with God up or down?

I love this question. Consider the acceleration of a jet engine behind your situation. You could be really soaring soon, or you could be headed for a mangling crash. The situation can get out of hand before you know it.

> **Without a relationship with God connecting your efforts to God's power, the dreams He has placed in your heart are likely to spiral into a big mess.**

You are the pilot of your life. You have the choice to bolt full throttle and pull up the nose of the plane. God is the engine, the power, and the glory in your life. Your job is to reach out and to trust in Him. Most of us, however, get confused. We presume we are the pilot and the power. That's where things turn terribly wrong. This is where aspirations nose-dive out of control.

Although you are certainly the navigator of your future, you are not the engine behind your dreams. Your relationship with God is. It connects you to the heart of God so your life can be fueled continually by God's power. God is the source making possible the desires of your heart. First Corinthians 8:3, *"But the man who loves*

God is known by God."
Without a relationship
with God connecting
your efforts to God's
power, the work He has
placed in your heart is
likely to spiral into a big
mess.

In fact, it is through
all of your relationships

> **It's through
> your intimate
> relationship
> with Jesus that
> will deliver
> soaring results.**

that results are derived. When your marriage prospers
and your spouse believes in you, trust me, you can
conquer the world. Imagine the alternative. When your
kids are troubled or other key relationships are strained,
where will your mind be consumed? Can you function
at your best under these conditions and continue to
strive for your dreams?

God is wisdom. Without the Word and communication with Him, you lack true wisdom. You are
a plane without an engine. If you are not listening to
and looking for His direction, how can God direct your
steps? Absent God's truth, the enemy will shoot down
your hopes and purpose with discouraging lies, delays,
or failure.

Many people desire to know God's purpose for
their life, but they feel stuck and unsure because their
relationship with Him is not active and alive. They don't
feel they are hearing from God or don't know how;
therefore, they do nothing. In reality, this decision to "do

nothing" is actually doing something. It is following the path of least resistance, which leads to living life in a rut—without hope, without faith. When you fall into a rut and decide to stay there, your relationship with God is no longer growing, either.

Stuck is not only a book about becoming a dreamer again and achieving the hopes God has for you. It is about nurturing the important relationships in your life, starting with your connection with God. It's about pulling you out of the rut and helping you aspire to something. Because when you work toward the vision God has placed in your heart, you are automatically seeking a closer relationship with Him. What you pursue is less important than the pursuit itself. We all know that striving for anything beyond our own abilities (e.g., fighting a giant, walking on water, etc.) will cause our relationship with God to deepen. It is this deepening relationship with God that will actually deliver the results we are after.

> **Relationships yield results. Results do not yield relationships.**

When you are making progress, it can be easy to become more focused on the work than on God. It's tragic to let results get ahead of the relationship. To prevent that from happening, keep your finger on the pulse of your relationship with God. The enemy is out to kill, steal, and destroy you and create a barrier to living out your dream by making you results-focused rather than relationship-focused.

Relationships yield results. Results do not yield relationships. There is probably not a single success in your life that was not made possible through a key relationship. Every venture you pursue will reflect the key relationships in your life. If you yell at your wife, then that same rage exists at the office. If you have trouble with managing your finances at home today, this condition will show up in your hobby or any other pursuit. However, if your home life is a source of constant encouragement, you will be a source of life to everyone with whom you come in contact. If your heart is filled with the knowledge of who God is and who you are in Christ, there is not a lie in this world or a pot-shot from the enemy that can bring you down. Keep the relationship engines tuned up and the nose of your life plane will continue to soar toward your accomplishing all God has for you.

> *"Be assured, if you walk with Him and look to Him, and expect help from Him, He will never fail you."*
> ~ GEORGE MUELLER

Maybe you recognize that you do not yet have a personal relationship with God. Maybe you have been focused on your life—going your way and doing it all on your own. If that's the case, everything you do will eventually lead to destruction. Matthew 7:13, *"Enter through the narrow gate. For wide is the gate and broad is the road that leads to destruction, and many enter through it."*

"Enter into the promises of God. It is your inheritance."

~ SMITH WIGGLESWORTH

If you are ready to invite Him into your life, Acts 16:31 says, *"Believe in the Lord Jesus, and you will be saved."* Simply believe and confess with your mouth that Jesus Christ is your Lord. Ask Him to place His Holy Spirit in you. If you are not sure of your salvation or you do not know what to say to God, pray this prayer:

> *Father. I am sorry for my sins. I believe that Jesus took the punishment for my sin on the cross. I believe you love me. I believe Jesus died to forgive my sins. I receive that forgiveness. Jesus, I make you my Lord. I believe that you are alive and that you now live in me. I am saved. I am forgiven. Thank*

you that I am born again. Thank you that I am the temple of the Holy Spirit. Father, I welcome your Holy Spirit to fill me from head to toe with your power and your knowledge. I receive all the gifts your Spirit offers. I give you my life. Thank you for loving me and giving me new life. I trust that I am yours and am now sealed with your Spirit! In Jesus name, amen.

You are now in Christ! You are His child. Don't doubt it. Are you unsure? Romans 10:13, *"Everyone who calls on the name of the Lord will be saved."* That includes you. Do not look back. Walk forward with the Father from now on! Leave your old life of sin and rebellion because you have been made new, clean, and holy! Welcome to the family of God!

But seek first his kingdom and his righteousness, and all these things will be given to you as well.
~ MATTHEW 6:33

With the completion of this book, I am able to pull down this dream from my personal *Stickie Dreamwall*. I am no longer *Stuck*! Thank you for sharing in this experience with me!

**Delight yourself in the Lord
and He will give you the desires
of your heart.**

~ PSALM 37:4

iKAN Ministries

Watch the Stickie Dreamwall video at our website www.ikanministries.com/stuck.html
Tools to Know God More and Know Who You Are in Him!
Become a Lie Spy, free Bible study, Live Prayer, Worship, Audio Healing Verses, and more
www.ikanministries.com

SOAR Bible Study

Boot camp to knowing God more intimately – a free Bible study.
www.soarwithgod.com

Truth or Trash iPhone App

Find this App in the iTunes Store or at ikanministries.com/truthortrash.html

Truth or Trash Card Game

http://www.mardel.com/Truth-Or-Trash-Card-Game-All-Ages-3023686.aspx
http://www.amazon.com/Truth-Trash-Card-Game-Original/dp/B00EW4APNC
www.ikanministries.com/truthortrash.html

Our Church Home

Lifechurch.tv Worship online from anywhere!

Find more information from those who helped with and are in this book:

Trisha Heddlesten	communicateclearlyokc.com
Micah Marie Photography	micahmariephotography.com
Amy Groeschel	amygroeschel.wordpress.com
Marcy Priest	marcypriest.com
Cheli Porter	twitter.com/chelip
Stephanie Davis-Reed	twitter.com/stephldavis5128
Jemma Stemmons	twitter.com/jemmastemmons

Made in the
USA
Monee, IL